1993
1993

1870–1970
Century of Growth in English Education

1870–1970

Century of Growth
in English Education

H. C. Dent

Foreword by Sir John Newsom

LONGMAN

LONGMAN GROUP LIMITED
London

*Associated companies, branches and representatives
throughout the world*

© Longman Group Ltd 1970

First published 1970

SBN 582 32805 5 paper edition
SBN 582 32804 7 cased edition

*Printed in Great Britain by
Spottiswoode, Ballantyne and Co Ltd,
London and Colchester*

Foreword

I am glad to commend this survey of a century of growth in English education not only because the century records, particularly in its first and last quarters, a quite remarkable development, but because its author has been, though his modesty would refuse the tribute, one of the major influences in the past thirty years. Harold Dent is uniquely qualified by scholarship and experience to describe the events since the Act of 1870. A pupil in an elementary school at the turn of the century (if only some of the obscurantist critics of our contemporary primary schools had 'enjoyed' this experience!) he had been Headmaster, Professor of Education and Editor of our most distinguished educational journal. He has travelled widely at home and abroad and *seen* what happens in schools and higher education as well as reading the voluminous, and frequently tedious literature of the subject. His books, some of which he lists in his bibliography, have had a marked effect both as history and even more as prophecy and exhortation. No man is more competent to write this book than he, and to make readable a story which is so often made incomprehensible by arcane expression and a jargon more loathsome and unnecessary than most.

Professor Dent admits, as common sense demands, that we are still a long way from the fulfilment of the ideals which inspired those responsible for the succession of Education Acts since 1870. Education is still concerned with establishing basic literacy, numeracy and oracy, rather than with the full education of each child's potential ability. It is still not a real *national* system for all our children even though all but a small minority are within its framework. The products of that minority still control the nodal points of power, whether it be in policy, finance or curriculum and *their* children, or more frequently their grandchildren, are unaffected by the system's deficiency. A slender acquaintance, for example, with those who govern the Scandinavian schools reveals a different attitude. Teachers and administrators *there* refer to the schools as 'our' schools and their pupils are not 'they' as opposed to 'us'. Nevertheless, the advance in the last twenty-five years has secured the commanding heights and, unless we foolishly throw away this advantage, enlightened, progressive education should steadily increase.

Problems abound and require no repetition; Professor Dent indicates those which are most important and, sadly, the most difficult to solve. Enough adequately educated and vocationally prepared teachers; buildings and equipment suitable for their purpose, the constant examination and modification of the curriculum and the preservation of professional and parental freedom within a publicly financed and controlled system.

Having said the obvious, it is yet true that we should not despair because, in a hundred years, we have not achieved what has only recently been held to be the ideal. Even a superficial reading of the intentions of those who secured the passing of the Education Acts from 1870 to 1936 shows the dramatic qualitative difference which inspired the Act of 1944. Yet, as Professor Dent reminds us, the 1944 Act was designed 'to reform' rather than to begin afresh. Indeed the latter would have been quite impracticable. All educational growth stems from established roots and even the Act of 1870 had its seeds sown at least fifty years earlier. Professor Dent has given us his survey, factual but, mercifully, far from dispassionate.

Those responsible might well, indeed, use it as an inspiration for the next stages, for unless and until the Apollyon of ignorance and deprivation is challenged in the spirit of Mr Valiant for Truth rather than of Mr Faint Heart we shall not enter the Delectable Mountains. All the trumpets sounded for Mr Standfast when he went down into the river—they sounded, I believe, in harmony. Today, at times, 'the trumpets flourish up and down but give no sound at all'. Only on a sustained note can the forces be rallied to construct an England worthy of its young, a City of God rather than a City of Destruction.

John Newsom

Contents

Illustrations

Preface

This book is an enlargement of the three Joseph Payne Memorial Lectures which, at the invitation of the College of Preceptors, I gave in 1967.

I chose the topic because I was becoming increasingly alarmed by the incessant complaints I heard and read about the defects and deficiencies of the English educational system. What really touched me on the raw was the allegation, repeated over and over again, and no doubt sincerely believed, that 'conditions have never been worse'. I began to think of my own schooldays, and especially of the three public elementary schools I attended between 1900 and 1904. From there my thoughts went back to the era of Joseph Payne, and Robert Lowe's Revised Code, when my mother (one of the more fortunate children of her age) was paying her weekly pence to be taught the '3 Rs', and plain needlework, in a pre-1870 elementary school.

I determined to try to give in my lectures some idea of how far we have travelled in English education since those days. Inevitably, my achievement fell short of my hopes. So the invitation from John Newsom, a friend of long standing whose work in education I had admired for thirty years, to expand the lectures into a book was very welcome. Now the book is done I am left with the same feeling of insufficiency. How difficult it is to do justice in words to even one aspect of a century crowded with events!

I hope the foregoing paragraphs make clear that this book is very far from being a comprehensive history of education in England and Wales between 1870 and 1970. It is simply an attempt to show that our educational services, whatever their shortcomings today, have during that century been developed, diversified, and improved almost out of recognition. As such, it is a highly selective account. I do not ignore the innumerable errors, omissions, feeblenesses and failures that have marred our policy and practice during the century, but except in the last chapter (which deals with current, and therefore remediable, trends) I do not go out of my way to highlight them. I emphasize our triumphs rather than our tragedies.

This attitude may seem to some people intolerably complacent. I would deny the charge. In my opinion we dwell too much upon our failings; all I seek to do is to redress the balance. We have done many good things in education, have scored many signal successes. I have myself witnessed many notable achievements, through having been almost continuously involved in English education—as pupil, teacher, journalist, and then teacher again—during nearly three-quarters of the century I here describe. I am proud to have known large numbers of the men and women who helped to bring them about. Not all of these people are known to fame; most, indeed, are not. But their foresight, their faith, and their courage live on in the advances they made. To them, to those who are following in their footsteps today, and to those who will do so tomorrow, I dedicate this book.

H. C. Dent

Part One

Building a National System

I

Filling Gaps

We must make up our minds to see the last of him, as far as the day school is concerned, at 10 or 11. We must frame our system of education upon this hypothesis; and I venture to maintain that it is quite possible to teach a child soundly and thoroughly, in a way that he shall not forget it, all that it is necessary for him to possess in the shape of intellectual attainment, by the time that he is ten years old.

Rev. James Fraser, to the Newcastle Commission, 1861.[1]

It can hardly be denied that England was in the 1860s one of the worst educated countries in the West. Nor could its condition be expected to improve while views such as those of Mr Fraser (an Oxford don, shortly to become a bishop) remained sufficiently influential to induce Ministers of the Crown to act upon them—as did Robert Lowe, Vice-President of the Committee of the Privy Council on Education, when in 1862 he imposed upon the English elementary school a 'Revised' Code of Regulations which in effect restricted its curriculum to the '3 Rs' and lowered its leaving age to eleven.

But Fraser and Lowe, and all who thought like them, were rowing against the tide of their times. Lowe implicitly acknowledged this in 1867, when Disraeli's famous 'leap into the dark'—the Representation of the People Act—forced him to repudiate his former beliefs. This Act practically doubled the number of parliamentary voters, and in particular gave the vote to great numbers of working-class men in the large towns. Lowe fought the Bill furiously from first to last; but when came up for its Third Reading showed his statesmanship by recognizing its social implications. In a memorable speech, which in quotation is usually telescoped into the five words, 'We must educate our masters', he said:

> It appears to me that before we had intrusted the masses—the great bulk of whom are uneducated—with the whole power of this

3

country we should have taught them a little more how to use it, and not having done so, this rash and abrupt measure [the Representation of the People Act] having been forced upon them, *the only thing we can do is as far as possible to remedy the evil by the most universal measures of education that can be devised. I believe it will be absolutely necessary that you should prevail on our future masters to learn their letters. . . . From the moment that you intrust the masses with power their education becomes an absolute necessity.*[2]

A host of more discerning observers—Matthew Arnold, Thomas Carlyle, Charles Dickens, William Edward Forster, Thomas Henry Huxley, John Stuart Mill, Lyon Playfair, John Ruskin, to name but a few of Lowe's contemporaries—had long foreseen this. Some had even suspected that mere 'letters'—the rudiments of literacy—might not suffice even the 'labouring poor' in the more scientific and technological age being brought to birth by such men as Bessemer, Brunel, Darwin and Lister. And not only such prophets, but also increasing numbers of ordinary people had grown more and more perturbed about the nation's education, and had in various ways made clear their deep dissatisfaction with every part of it.

Mid-century reforms

This mounting volume of protest had produced some impressive reforms. In the 1850s Royal Commissions had recommended, and Acts of Parliament implemented, a radical modernization of the ancient universities of Oxford and Cambridge. In the 1860s other Royal Commissions had dealt similarly with the aristocratic 'Public' schools and the heterogeneous mass of Endowed schools. The recommendations of these Commissions, too, had been followed by Acts of Parliament, not so drastic as those reforming the universities, but one of them at any rate, the Endowed Schools Act 1869, productive of long-term results of the utmost importance. It is merely speculative to suggest that this Act started England off on the long road which led ultimately to secondary education for all; it is certain that it started secondary education on a substantial scale for girls, hitherto denied it except in a few courageously unorthodox schools.

In the vast post-school territory known today as Further Education enterprising pioneers had launched a wide variety of projects. At South Kensington the Science and Art Department had started courses and examinations for teachers as well as for pupils. Christian Socialists had established adult colleges for working-class folk in such unlikely spots as Sheffield and St Pancras. At Manchester a college of higher education had been built with money bequeathed by a wool merchant who had actually dreamed—presumptuously, as many people felt—that it might one day become a university. Even more presumptuously, a woman called Emily Davies, who had been active in every campaign for the betterment of girls' education since the 1840s, had recently dug herself in at Hitchin, not far from Cambridge, with a female commando of six students preposterously intended to breach the masculine ramparts of that city's ancient university and wrest from the male species its immemorial monopoly of entry therein.

But such ventures—and there were others—could benefit only the fortunate few whom favourable circumstances, or extreme persistence, had rendered intellectually capable of profiting from them. A great mass of English people still lacked the indispensable foundation for advanced studies: a sound elementary education. Like the secondary schools and universities, the elementary schools had had their Royal Commission, the Newcastle Commission of 1858–61; but, unlike the others, this had not been followed by legislation, only by regulation. And, shockingly unlike the others, the measures taken had been designed to restrain rather than reform.

Elementary education for all

By 1870, however, the stark necessity for making elementary education available to all, and everywhere efficient, was generally acknowledged. But how, and by whom, it should be provided remained unsolved problems. During the 1860s alone, half a dozen parliamentary Bills had perished in the attempt to find an agreed solution—as had many others previously. All had died in the flames of sectarian strife. In 1869, when it had become clear that the recently installed Liberal Government was determined to put an Education Act on the Statute Book, this strife reached a new peak of intensity as the warring factions mobilized under the hostile banners of the National Education Union, pledged to preserve denominational schools, and the predominance of the Church of England, and the National Education League, pledged to rid the nation's schools ultimately of all denominational taint, and to make elementary education unsectarian, free, compulsory, and universal.

Despite the apparent impossibility of reconciling these antagonistic attitudes, one common conviction gradually imposed itself upon most thoughtful minds. Voluntary effort alone was not enough. Even Edward Baines of Leeds, for many years the leader of the dyed-in-the-

5

wool Voluntaryists, had, in 1867, been forced to acknowledge this. In 1869 the Annual Report of the Committee of Council on Education, in cumbrous language, officially confirmed this widespread belief.

In order that our administration should, within any reasonable period, attain to the dimensions of a national system, by which the means of efficient elementary education may be brought within the reach of every home, some further and powerful impulse must be given to its working. *That impulse must plainly be sought outside and beyond the benevolent energy of the small body of volunteers on whose co-operation we have hitherto relied* (pp. vii, viii; *italics mine*).

In blunter words, a haphazard scatter of schools provided and maintained solely by voluntary bodies, even though supported by government subsidy, could no longer satisfy even the minimum educational demands of England's increasingly industrial society. In numerous heavily populated districts there were no schools. In some large cities the situation was desperate. 'As a Liverpool magistrate', Mr Melly told the House of Commons: 'I assert that there are from 25,000 to 30,000 children in the streets of Liverpool who are learning nothing, if they be not learning habits of vagrancy, mendicancy, and crime.'[3]

Spurred on by Mr Melly and other MPs, the government ordered an inquiry, and the Education Department sent two experienced HMIs, the Reverend D. R. Fearon and Mr J. G. (later Sir Joshua) Fitch, to Birmingham, Leeds, Liverpool and Manchester. They reported[4] that of just under a quarter of a million children between the ages of five and thirteen in these cities, 118,000—nearly half—were not attending any school.

(It should be made very clear what 'not attending any school' could mean at that time. In large towns thousands of children were homeless 'street arabs'. And in town and countryside alike:

. . . the child in the 'sixties was still the victim of the most dangerous, the most wearing, and the most exposed occupations. The insatiable demand for child labour, the inhuman doctrines of political economy, and the evil conditions of industrial life were still united in imposing upon the young . . . terrible sufferings.[5]

Not until 1867 was the employment of children under eight totally forbidden in factories, not until 1873 the employment of children under ten in gangs on farms—and even then eight-year-olds could be employed who had made 250 attendances at school during the preceding year. (It must be added that all the laws purporting to regulate the employment of children were widely evaded.)

Of the 132,000 who were attending school, fewer than 80,000—not much over half—were in schools that were grant-aided (and therefore inspected) by the Committee of Council on Education. Of the uninspected (i.e. private) schools in Manchester Mr Fearon wrote that:

> Many . . . are held in premises in which it is injurious and improper that human beings should be gathered together for any purpose whatever, and in which instruction is physically impossible. The teachers of many of them are persons physically, morally, or intellectually disqualified for any office, involving even the lowest degree of responsibility. The instruction given, or pretended to be given, in them is deplorably bad; and attendance at many of them is scarcely, if at all, to be preferred to vagrancy or truancy in the streets.

In Liverpool, said Mr Fearon, 'The quality of the education is, on the whole, worse in the uninspected schools . . . than in . . . Manchester'. Such generalized strictures, which were paralleled by those of Mr Fitch about Birmingham and Leeds, were amply documented by detailed descriptions of individual schools. Two examples may perhaps suffice.

> LEEDS. In a squalid little room 14 feet 4 inches by 8 feet, in a back street, I [Mr Fitch] found, on descending to the basement floor of a small house, thirty-three children crowded together, of whom sixteen were boys. The master is standing, in his shirt sleeves near the fire, over which some stew is preparing for dinner. The room is hot and close, and the children move with difficulty, owing to the clumsiness of the household furniture with which it is nearly filled. [The master's] knowledge and qualifications are of the humblest kind, and his method of instruction is to hear the lessons of each child one by one, while the rest are 'learning off their spellings'.

For this travesty of education pupils paid fourpence a week—no inconsiderable sum in days when one could 'get drunk for a penny and blind drunk for twopence'. Those scholars who added writing (in copybooks) to the meagre curriculum paid sixpence. 'No other written or memory exercises are given', records Mr Fitch, 'and the children are deplorably inactive and ignorant.' No wonder. Apart from any other consideration, even had the room not been 'nearly filled' with furniture, had it in fact been completely empty, its dimensions allowed barely $3\frac{1}{2}$ square feet per person for the master and his thirty-three pupils. And this was by no means the worst hovel masquerading as a school which was discovered by the two HMIs.

LIVERPOOL. This cellar has two parts, front and back. The front cellar is approached from the street by a flight of stone steps, and is lighted by a small window below the level of the street. . . . The back cellar is not lighted at all, or, apparently, paved or floored in any way. In these two cellars the master says he has sometimes had as many as eighty children . . .

To anyone studying this Report a century after its publication, what is even more profoundly shocking than the fact that such conditions existed is to discover that they were tolerated—or ignored—by organized Christian communities. Mr Fitch sadly commented that in Leeds: 'With the exception of the Wesleyans and the Unitarians, I have been unable to find a single Nonconformist congregation . . . which is doing anything to help forward primary education, or is contributing money, or supervision, to the permanent maintenance of a day school in any form.' He implied much the same about some at least of the Anglican congregations. The only Church which, as a matter of policy, required every one of its congregations to contribute regularly to the support of its schools was the Roman Catholic—despite the fact that it was hampered by the abject poverty of many of its communities, notably in Liverpool, the West Riding of Yorkshire, and some districts in the London area where, as in the north, there was a heavy concentration of Irish immigrants.

Voluntary effort alone was manifestly not enough. There were two alternatives: to replace it completely by statutory provision, or to supplement it by such provision. Replacement, that is, the abolition of voluntary schools, though strongly urged by extreme anti-denominationalists, was in 1870, as always before, politically a non-starter. Supplementation was the only practicable strategy; and it was this that the Minister for Education had to sell to Parliament.

William Edward Forster

England was extremely fortunate in the man to whom was entrusted the task of reconciling the conflicting claims of Church and State and of piloting through Parliament the country's first Education Act. William Edward Forster, whom Gladstone appointed in 1868 Vice-President of the Committee of Council on Education, was a middle-class mid-Victorian Liberal of the best kind. He combined in his rugged personality the finer characteristics of three notable traditions:

8

the religious integrity of the Society of Friends; the Benthamite urge
to social reform; and the hard-headed business acumen of the Yorkshire wool merchant. He was by descent a Quaker. His father was a
much-loved peripatetic Quaker preacher, and a leader in the struggle
to abolish slavery. (He died on a missionary visit to the American
plantations.) His mother, a Buxton, belonged to the élite inner circle
of Quaker families. Yet Forster had the courage to accept expulsion
from the Society of Friends as the penalty for marrying a wife who was
not a Quaker: Jane Arnold, daughter of Thomas Arnold of Rugby,
and sister of Matthew. Matthew Arnold's intimate knowledge of
education in England and in European countries was invaluable to
Forster during his years as Minister for Education. But Forster's
enlightened attitude towards public education, and his belief that it
should be provided by statutory bodies, had been formed many years
previously. In the early 1840s, as a young man just embarking on a
business career in Bradford, he was already insisting on 'the right of
the English working man to demand an education for his children—
such an education as could only be obtained through the action of the
State'.[6]

Both before and after his election in 1861 as Member of Parliament
for Bradford he was prominent among those who 'advocated the
establishment of a national system'.[7] Doubtless his experiences in
1864–8 as a member of the Schools Inquiry Commission, which laid
bare the deplorable state of secondary education, did nothing to
weaken this conviction. Certainly, when he became Vice-President of
the Committee of Council on Education he made it clear that he
'would support no measure that was merely voluntary, either as
regards the provision of schools or the attendance of scholars'.[8] On
the other hand, he flatly rejected the demand for a wholly statutory
system. This would, he told the Cabinet in a memorandum outlining
his legislative proposals, 'quickly undermine the existing schools,
would relieve the parents of all payment, would entail upon the
country an enormous expense, and—a far more dangerous loss than
that of money—would drive out of the field most of those who cared
for education'.[9] Instead, Forster advised the Government to adopt a
plan (ironically, recently proposed by Robert Lowe) whereby it
would make a national survey of needs, give the voluntary bodies a
specified period of time in which to remedy deficiencies, and then,
wherever they had not done so, move in and do the job itself.

That during the exhausting parliamentary battles over his Education Bill, which raged for five months, from February to August 1870,
Forster never abandoned that standpoint, whatever other concessions

9

he made, is certainly a tribute to his moral rectitude; but it is equally a tribute to his physical and mental toughness and his parliamentary expertise. His moral rectitude has been frequently applauded by historians; but many appear to overlook the fact that Forster was an able and experienced politician as well as an educational idealist. Had he not been, he would never have got his Bill through; it would have been killed or mangled like all the others. But he was wise enough to placate his parliamentary critics by making four crucial changes in it before it entered the Committee stage of detailed scrutiny.

1. His proposed 'School Boards' would be elected by direct ballot of the rate-payers, and not, as he had proposed, by the Borough councils and parish Vestries.

2. No denominational religious instruction would be allowed in Board schools (the famous 'Cowper-Temple' clause). Originally, Forster had proposed that School Boards should decide whether or not religious instruction would be given in their schools.

3. No financial aid from local rates would be given to denominational schools. Rate-aid had been promised in the Bill as originally presented to Parliament. By way of compensation, denominational schools could be given up to 50 per cent more Exchequer grant than previously.

4. The original Bill included a 'Conscience Clause', under which, by application in writing, parents could withdraw their children from religious instruction in school. In place of this Clause, a more precise 'Timetable Conscience Clause' was substituted which laid down that religious instruction was to be given only during the first or the last period of the school day—thus ensuring that no one missed any of the secular instruction.

Disraeli, the leader of the Opposition, said that these changes virtually made it a new Bill. Strategically they did, but they did not compromise Forster's objective: efficient elementary education available everywhere for everyone.

'On the whole', wrote James Macdonell, a well-known journalist, to a friend in 1870, 'I think Forster has hit on the only plan that will work in so curious a country as England'.[10] What exactly was that plan, as it emerged from Parliament, and how well did it work?

Aims of 1870 Act

In the memorandum which Forster prepared for the Cabinet in 1869, and which formed the basis of the Bill he introduced into the House of Commons on 17 February 1870, he declared that: 'Our aim, then, must be (1) to cover the country with good schools, and (2) to get the parents to send their children to those schools.'[11]

How formidable a task the first aim involved Forster made terribly clear in his speech introducing the Bill, when he enumerated the deficiencies in the existing provision of elementary education. He pointed out[12] that, while the names of some 1,450,000 children were entered in the registers of the 13,000 elementary schools (11,000 day schools, 2,000 night schools) that were inspected and grant-aided by the Government, 'only two-fifths of the children of the working classes between the ages of six and ten . . . and only one-third of those between the ages of ten and twelve' were included in that number. This meant, in round figures, that 'of those between six and ten, we have helped about 700,000 . . . but we have left unhelped 1,000,000; while of those between ten and twelve, we have helped 250,000, and left unhelped at least 500,000'. Even this depressing statement gave an over-rosy picture of the actual situation. For while there were nearly a million and a half names *on the registers* of the grant-aided schools, the *average attendance* of pupils at those schools was only about a million.

In addition to the inspected schools, there were also, said Forster, the uninspected. He had not forgotten these. But, he added, they were 'the worst schools . . . the least fitted to give a good education to the children of the working classes'.[13]

Such was the situation. 'What are the results?' asked Forster, and bluntly replied: 'What we might have expected.'

Much imperfect education and much absolute ignorance; good schools become bad schools for children who attend them for only a few weeks in the year; and though we have done well in assisting the benevolent gentlemen who have established schools, yet the result of the State leaving the initiative to volunteers, is, that where State help has been most wanted, State help has been least given, and that where it was desirable that State power should be most felt it was not felt at all.

Consequently:

. . . notwithstanding the large sums of money we have voted, we find a vast number of children badly taught, or utterly untaught, because there are too few schools and too many bad schools, and because there are large numbers of parents in this country who cannot, or will not, send their children to school.[14]

To appreciate the full gravity of that indictment it is essential to realize that it was uttered by someone whose educational thinking, though in some respects rather in advance of that of most English people in 1870, was not greatly so. In other respects Forster was very much a product of his times. There can be, I think, little doubt that in this speech his reactions to the state of the schools, and the attitude of parents, represented those of the bulk of sober and thoughtful middle-class folk. He was, that is, assessing the educational situation in the light of 1870 standards—standards which to 1970 minds seem almost unbelievably unexacting.

A similar reminder must be given about the Education Act to which Forster gained the assent of both Houses of Parliament in 1870. To some of us, looking at it a hundred years later, it may well appear to be a crude, timid, compromising measure. But to probably the majority of Forster's contemporaries (as to Forster himself) it was bold to the point of being revolutionary. To many people it seemed desperately dangerous. Compromise it certainly was; but what must be remembered is that in order to get any Education Act on to the Statute Book which infringed the near-monopoly of the Church of England, and granted to public authorities any degree of control over elementary education, Forster had to do what a long line of politicians —from Samuel Whitbread in 1807 down to himself in 1868—had failed to do: to produce a measure to which he could get the State, the Established Church, the various bodies of Nonconformists, the Secularists, and the Voluntaryists, to agree. And that was by no means the only obstacle—though by far the most formidable—that he had to overcome. He had also to overcome, or at least to soften up, the hostility of employers accustomed for generations to exploiting the cheap labour of children, and of parents accustomed—often by sad necessity —to relying on the money which that cheap labour brought in; to contend with the parsimony of a Government whose dominating financial aim seemed to be to reduce taxation; and to induce Parliament to accept a principle which it had in the past consistently rejected: that of subsidizing public education from local rates as well as national taxes. Only when all these points are borne in mind can one fully flavour that key passage in Forster's speech in which he circumspectly defined his Government's intentions:

> Our object is to complete the present voluntary system, to fill up gaps, sparing the public money where it can be done without, procuring as much as we can the assistance of the parents, and welcoming as much as we rightly can the co-operation and aid of those benevolent men who desire to assist their neighbours.[15]

Again and again in his speech Forster makes conciliatory gestures towards interested parties from whom he is going to demand sacrifices, of conscience, or pocket, or both. For example, in discussing his aim to cover the country with good schools, he suggests that there are 'certain conditions which I think honorable members on both sides of the House will acknowledge we must abide by'. . . . 'We must not forget the duty of the parents . . . our duty to our constituencies, our duty to the taxpayers . . . we must take care not to destroy in building up—not to destroy the existing system in introducing a new one.'[16]

The function of the local School Boards proposed in his Bill was to be strictly limited to filling any gaps left by voluntary effort. Forster was quite definite about this. England and Wales, he explained, were to be divided into 'school districts', based on borough and civil parish boundaries. All the districts would be scrutinized 'to ascertain their educational condition', that is, to discover the extent of the existing provision of schools and the quality of the education being given. Then, he promised: 'If in any one of these districts we find the elementary education to be *sufficient, efficient, and suitable*, we leave that district alone'.[17]

The primary responsibility, therefore, lay with the Voluntary School Managers and the religious bodies under whose aegis most of them were functioning. If they could show that the education they were providing in their district was 'sufficient, efficient, and suitable', or that if it was not they would undertake to make it so within a specified period of time, they would remain, as previously, the sole providers. Admittedly, in any districts where the existing provision did not satisfy Forster's criteria, the school authorities would have to make swift decisions. The time to be allowed them was drastically cut during the parliamentary debates. It was originally intended to be twelve months; it was reduced to under five. The Bill became law on 9 August; the deadline for decision, and for submission to the Committee of Council of proposals for improvement, was the end of December.

Prodigious expansion

Be it said at once that most of them rose magnificently to the challenge. Within the five months' 'period of grace' they submitted to the Education Department 3,342 applications for building grants—more than they had sent in during the whole of the previous twenty years. Alas! in many cases the gesture proved too magnificent; over one-third (1,333) of these applications were later withdrawn, and a further 376 were rejected by the Department. Nevertheless, the astonishing fact remains that within ten years the voluntary bodies nearly doubled the

13

numbers of their schools, their pupils and their teachers. The Church of England, much the largest provider, increased the number of its schools from nearly 6,400 to over 11,400, of pupils in average attendance from under 850,000 to over 1,470,000, and of Certificated teachers from 9,600 to 18,600. The Roman Catholics more than doubled the number of their schools and of their pupils: from 350 to 758, and from 66,000 to 145,000 respectively. (The British and Foreign School Society adopted the policy of transferring schools in financial difficulty to the School Boards, and so increased their numbers to a much smaller extent.)

Admittedly, school buildings were far less sophisticated (if often more solid) then than now, and so could be put up much more quickly and cheaply. Admitted also that the large increases in the number of grant-earning schools, and of places in such schools, were not by any means due entirely to the building of new schools; many existing premises could be sufficiently improved by 'minor works' to qualify for grant, and many schools not previously grant-aided applied for and secured recognition. Admit further that the *average attendance* made by the four million *on the registers* of the grant-earning schools in 1880 was well under three million. But when every reservation is made, the expansion of the public elementary school between 1870 and 1880 can only be described as a prodigious feat.

To this vast expansion the School Boards, particularly those in the large towns, made a substantial contribution. By 1880 they had built or acquired over 3,400 schools, in which the average attendance exceeded 750,000. But to get the picture in perspective it is essential to realize that not only during this decade but throughout the thirty years' life of the Boards there were more children in Voluntary schools than in Board schools. In 1880 the Voluntary schools still contained over 70 per cent of public elementary school pupils, in 1890 over 60 per cent, and as late as 1900 nearly 55 per cent. The fundamental importance of the School Boards' contribution—or at any rate of the large urban Boards—lay in its quality. From the start these Boards set the standards: in buildings, in equipment, and in staffing. They could do so because they had at their command an ample and *unfailing* source of revenue denied to the Churches: the local rates. Upon the rates the Boards could precept at will, and no local authority could say them nay. (And a rare reputation for extravagance some Boards soon acquired, not all of them only in the eyes of their thriftier or more parsimonious rate-payers.) The Churches, like the Boards, had three main sources of income. Two of these were similar: government grant and pupils' fees. But against the School Boards' rates the Churches could pit only voluntary contributions and gifts; and though the amount these produced was doubled during the decade 1870–80, private philanthropy still could not measure up to public levy. In 1880, although the Exchequer grant was practically the same for a Voluntary as for a Board school, while Voluntary schools were on the whole charging rather higher fees, the average cost of a child in a Voluntary school was £1. 14s 7¾d, in a Board school £2. 1s 11¾d. By 1890 the gap had widened: £1. 16s 11½d in Voluntary schools, £2. 5s 11½d in Board schools.[18] By 1900 it had widened still more; not greatly, it is true, but inexorably, and this despite every device for fund-raising the Churches could employ. Moreover, from about 1885 more and more Voluntary schools got more and more heavily in debt. By 1900 their aggregate liabilities were said to exceed £450,000. The large School Boards could afford to put up more expensive buildings, and equip them more lavishly; to employ a larger proportion of certificated teachers, and pay them more highly; to indulge in educational experiments and innovations. Inevitably, this disparity in means was reflected in the quality of the work in the schools. Inevitably also the Churches pressed increasingly for more financial aid for Voluntary schools. And, unhappily, but no doubt inevitably, seeing what human nature is, the mutual antagonism between the Church of England, the principal champion of the Voluntary School, and the Protestant nonconformists, who by and large were supporters of the Board School, grew ever more bitter and intense.

Compulsory schooling

The financial security enjoyed by the School Boards was crucially important for the future of English education. So, too, was the power, conferred upon the Boards by Sec. 74 of the 1870 Act, to make bye-laws enforcing compulsory attendance at school throughout their districts. The history books all too often give the impression that it was Parliament which made elementary education compulsory: partially in 1876 and universally in 1880. But this is less than half the truth; compulsory education was brought about very largely by local—that is, School Board—action. What Parliament did was to give national sanction and support to local action already taken.

By the end of 1871 about 300 School Boards had been set up. Of these, 117 had already made bye-laws enforcing compulsory attendance, and had had these approved by the Education Department. Compulsion within very narrow limits, it is true. The London School Board, pioneer in this as in so many other matters throughout its thirty-year life, had passed a bye-law providing for compulsory

CENTURY OF GROWTH IN ENGLISH EDUCATION

attendance between the ages of five and thirteen—but allowing children over ten who had passed Standard V[19] to claim full exemption, that is, to leave school altogether, and children under ten to claim half-time exemption if they could be shown to be 'beneficially and necessarily' employed for the purpose of supporting themselves or their parents. Most of the other 116 bye-laws similarly allowed full exemption for children over ten and half-time exemption for younger children. But whereas London demanded a Standard V pass, some Boards were satisfied with Standard IV, and a few even with Standard III.

By 1873 four elementary school children out of every ten were attending compulsorily. In that year Parliament made its first move; it passed an Act imposing compulsory attendance on the children of parents in receipt of Poor Law relief. (Forster would have liked to bring in a Bill for general compulsion, but could not get all his Cabinet colleagues to agree.) By 1876 compulsory bye-laws covered half the elementary school population, but this aggregate concealed very great differences between urban and rural areas, and between School Board and Voluntary districts. In the large towns, run by progressive Boards, compulsion covered four-fifths of the children. This determined the Government—a Conservative Government by now—to act in a big way. The Education Act of 1876 provided that no child under ten could be employed, and no child between ten and fourteen unless he had either (a) passed a Standard IV examination in reading, writing, and arithmetic, and been given a 'Labour Certificate' by HM Inspector, or (b) made not fewer than 250 attendances during each of five years, at not more than two schools. (The latter soon became known as the 'Dunce's Certificate'.) The Act also confirmed the precedent—still observed in English educational legislation—which had been set by the bye-laws, of laying a statutory duty upon parents. Section 4 made universal 'the duty of the parent of every child to cause such child to receive efficient elementary instruction in reading, writing, and arithmetic', and followed this by the warning that 'if such parent fail to perform such duty he shall be liable to such orders and penalties as are provided by this Act'.

The warning was given force by the duty the Act laid upon the localities to establish authorities to administer its provisions: the School Boards where these existed, and in all other districts School Attendance Committees. But to balance the stick there was a carrot! The Education Department offered three years' free education to eleven-year-olds who had passed Standard IV and made at least 350 attendances during the two previous years.

16

The 1876 Act produced a fresh crop of bye-laws. By 1880 compulsion was well-nigh universal (97 per cent) in the large towns, though over the country as a whole it covered under three-quarters of the elementary school population. There also continued to be widespread evasion of the laws relating to the education and employment of children. The Government—a Liberal Government again—decided to enforce everywhere compulsory attendance at school. The Act introduced by Mr A. J. Mundella, Vice-President of the Committee of Council, required all School Boards and Attendance Committees which had not passed bye-laws enforcing compulsion to do so forthwith. Once more, this compulsion was within narrow limits; indeed, except for its universal application it was no improvement on 1876. No exemption could be granted to any child under ten. No exemption could be granted to a child between ten and thirteen unless he had reached the standard laid down in the bye-law. (This was the weak part of the Act; the standards prescribed varied enormously.)

Despite its limitations the 1880 Act registered a decision as fundamental in its way as that implied in the 1870 Act. In 1870 the State accepted a partial responsibility only: to fill up gaps. In 1880 it accepted a total responsibility: to ensure that every child received at least an elementary education. That this decision could be made so soon was a striking tribute not only to ten years' expansion of educational facilities but also to the progress of public opinion.

Broadening the curriculum

The 1870 Act had in ten years covered the country with schools. But Forster had promised not merely 'schools', he had promised 'good schools'. In respect of quality the decade hardly matched its achievements in quantity. This is perhaps hardly surprising, in view of the size and speed of the expansion. 'The accession of feeble schools and unwilling scholars', to use Charles Birchenough's words,[20] actually reduced for some years the percentage of scholars in average attendance; in 1870 it was 68·07, in 1875 below 67 per cent. One of the main purposes of the 1876 Act was to check this retrogression, to improve the average attendance. It was modestly successful in doing so; by 1880 the percentage had topped 70 per cent. But it is salutary to recall that in the years immediately preceding the introduction of the Revised Code it was nearly 75 per cent. The enforcement of a high standard of attendance involved an unceasing and persistent struggle over many years; as late as 1914 the average was still below 90 per cent. Not only did children play truant; parents and employers connived at illegal absence, and so also, to their shame, did some School Boards and School Attendance Committees; and even some magistrates.

To some degree—though this was not the primary reason—the unwillingness of children to attend school was due to the aridity of much of the instruction offered and the harsh, sometimes even brutal, disciplinary measures employed by many teachers facing huge and turbulent classes. In both respects amelioration was slow. The 1870 Act had said nothing about the curriculum; and this and subsequent Education Acts established the tradition that curricula and methods are not matters for parliamentary decision. The curriculum of the elementary school remained, however, throughout the nineteenth century very much a matter for decision by the Education Department, and it was by this means that the horrors of 'payment by results' were diminished, at first gradually, but later at greater speed. The Code of Regulations issued in 1871—the 'New Code', as it was called —began the trend towards a more liberal curriculum by offering a grant (of three shillings a head) for a pass in not more than two 'specific subjects'. A relatively minor concession, for specific subjects could be taken only by children in the top three standards, and the grant was only three-quarters of that for a pass in one of the '3 Rs'. The first beginnings of a real breakthrough came in 1875, when 'class subjects' were introduced. To qualify for grant, these had to be taught to all the children in the school above Standard I. A 'good' pass in any two class subjects earned 4s a head, a 'fair' pass 2s. At the same time the grant for specific subjects was raised to 4s, while that for the '3 Rs' was reduced from 4s to 3s—a sure sign that the centre of gravity in the curriculum was shifting. Unhappily, both class and specific subjects lent themselves as readily to cramming and unintelligent memorization as did the '3 Rs'—thus leading to more 'payment by results': so much so that Professor Frank Smith claimed that the 1880s was the worst (though happily the last) period of this dreadful era. The last, because the advent in 1890 of a new Permanent Secretary at the Education Department, Sir George Kekewich, resulted in a rapid breaking down of the whole infamous system. By 1895 it was almost totally abolished—at least officially.

But alas! like John Brown's body—though infinitely less happily— its soul went marching on. I became a pupil in a public elementary school in 1900, some years after the last remnants of Lowe's Code had been officially removed, and I can testify from personal experience that the spirit inculcated by that Code was still very much in evidence in the attitudes and actions of both teachers and pupils. With relatively rare exceptions—I was most fortunate in one school—teachers and taught were sworn enemies. The latter resisted by every means known to them (and some of those means were extremely unpleasant) the desiccated diet of irrelevant facts the former persisted in pressing upon them; teachers retaliated with incessant applications of corporal punishment, impartially inflicted for crime, misdemeanour or mistake.

Teachers and pupil-teachers

This but illustrates tragically the truism that, whatever the system, the goodness or badness of the schools depends upon the teachers. In 1870 the outlook was not encouraging. Lowe's Revised Code had depressed the numbers, the quality, and the morale of the teachers. But the 1870 Act demanded, immediately, many more teachers, and the 'New Code' a higher proportion of certificated teachers, for it required that every school and department should be in the charge of a certificated teacher; at the time a requirement it was impossible to meet. Yet, despite the huge increase in the number of schools and pupils, by 1880 it was being more than met. But some of the expedients by which this result was achieved were, to say the least, a trifle dubious.

In 1870 the total teaching force in grant-aided schools was about 28,300. But of this number barely 12,500—considerably less than half —were certificated teachers. And a large proportion of these certificated teachers held only the Acting Teacher's Certificate, that is, they were not college-trained; they were ex-pupil-teachers who had secured a certificate by part-time study whilst serving as teachers, most of them as head teachers. The rest of the teaching force consisted almost entirely of pupil-teachers: over 14,500 of them. Up to 1870— and for long after in many schools—the normal staffing of a public elementary school was one head teacher and one or more pupil-teachers. Not until the London School Board began in 1873 to build schools 'on the Prussian plan, with a separate class room and teacher for each class'[21] did the adult assistant begin to replace the pupil-teacher. Separate classrooms were, indeed, one of the many causes of the decline and fall of the pupil-teacher system. In a single room the head could supervise simultaneously the work of all his pupil-teachers (and actually this was all that some heads did); but pupil-teachers tucked away in classrooms were another, and much more troublesome, matter.

London's experiment with classrooms, though soon copied by other large School Boards, did not prevent a rapid increase in the number of pupil-teachers: from 14,612 in 1870 to over 29,000 in 1875, over

32,000 in 1880. This was inevitable. There had to be more teachers, to man the schools, and the pupil-teacher system was virtually the only source of recruits. But by 1870 pupil-teachers were no longer regarded, as they had been in the 1850s, as the heaven-sent answer to HMIs' prayer. On the contrary, head teachers, training college staffs and inspectors alike were complaining about their low educational standard and their lack of teaching skill. Consequently, the swift increase in their number alarmed many certificated teachers, particularly as it was being accompanied by emergency measures which could hardly do other than lower professional standards—and so the teacher's status. The Committee of Council was encouraging training colleges (albeit 'with great reluctance') to pass out students after one year instead of the two that had been obligatory since 1856. Some colleges (Westminster was one) were actually sending out as many as half their students after such a shortened course. HMIs were being empowered to recommend the granting of the Certificate without examination to experienced serving teachers; and in the three years between December 1870 and December 1873 no fewer than twelve hundred such certificates were awarded. In 1874, and again in 1876, the standard required for HMIs' recommendation was lowered. So, too, was the pass standard in the training colleges—and one is bound to add that in the 1870s this was never very high. These were not exactly vintage years in most training colleges; in fact, there is reason for suspecting that never were their courses duller, their domestic life more dreary.

Largely by such measures, the number of teachers in grant-aided elementary schools was increased more than two and a half times between 1870 and 1880, as under.[22]

Description	1870	1880
Certificated teachers	12,467	31,422
Uncertificated 'assistant' teachers	1,262	7,652
Pupil-teachers	14,612	32,128
Total	28,341	71,202

In view of the concurrent massive increase in the number of schools and pupils, this increase in the number of teachers was not so good as it looks at first sight. The number of inspected elementary schools had risen from 8,281 in 1870 to 17,164 in 1880, and of pupils on their registers from about 1,850,000 to nearly four million. Numerically, the staffing situation had certainly improved, though not much. In respect of qualifications, and probably of teaching experience, it had deteriorated. Of the 31,422 certificated teachers about half were not college-trained. Among the 7,652 uncertificated assistants were 2,352 women who had no professional qualifications whatever. And pupil-teachers still remained the largest element in the teaching force. It is a sobering thought that throughout the public elementary school's first decade as a statutory institution it was very largely run by children between the ages of thirteen and eighteen.

By what seems an amazing omission (till one recalls the State Normal School row of 1839), the 1870 Act gave the School Boards no powers to train teachers. Nor did it restore to the training colleges the building grants of which they were deprived in 1863; or to head teachers the fees they had earned before the days of the Revised Code for tutoring their pupil-teachers.

The voluntary bodies did what they could about training colleges— and it was no inconsiderable bit. Proportionately, the British and Foreign School Society did most. By enlarging their long-established Borough Road (far and away the oldest training college in England), and Stockwell, its sister college, and by founding new colleges at Darlington and Swansea, the Society doubled within three years the number of their places. But set against the total number of training college places (or against the huge demand for teachers started by the 1870 Act), this did not, unfortunately, amount to very much. Even after its prodigious effort between 1871 and 1874, the BFSS was only providing about 15 per cent of the total number of training college places in England and Wales. The great majority—over two-thirds— was provided by the Church of England, which found anything approaching a doubling quite beyond its capacity. Consequently, though for the first time in their history all the training colleges were full, they were unable to admit in any year much over one-half of the pupil-teachers who had qualified for entry. As a result, the proportion of certificated teachers in the schools decreased between 1870 and 1880, and, owing to the emergency measures described above, the proportion of *trained* certificated teachers decreased substantially. And, however uninspired and ill-directed the average training college course may have been, at least it gave the ablest among the children preparing to be teachers a respite of two years from the rigours of teaching; and, for all the dreariness, narrowness, and overwork of college life, an opportunity along with one's fellows to become conscious, and proud, of belonging to a profession which, though it had no great social status had at least the compensation of being socially valuable.

But to large numbers of the teachers recruited to man the post-1870 schools this opportunity was denied; the training they received as pupil-teachers was the only training—other than the hard training of experience—which they ever received. And theirs was a task difficult beyond conception today—and that statement is made in full awareness of the conditions existing in the so-called 'jungle' schools of the 1960s. Far too little honour has been accorded to the elementary school teachers of the 1870s, who faced, and survived (and that was no mean feat), and in numerous instances positively triumphed over the formidable difficulties inherent in coping with an aggressively undisciplined 'first generation' of pupils, who were all too often aided and abetted in their indiscipline by everyone except their teachers. If the provision of school buildings between 1870 and 1880 was a near-miracle, the teachers' achievement in civilizing hordes of children who came unwillingly to school was even more so.

The School Boards had no powers to undertake the training of teachers. But some of them quickly began to undertake a task which in the long term was to prove equally valuable: improvement of the education of prospective teachers. In the year 1874-5 the Liverpool and London School Boards almost simultaneously began to assemble groups of pupil-teachers in 'pupil-teacher centres', specially housed, specially equipped, and specially staffed for giving general secondary education. The idea was not new. A voluntary centre of this kind (but on a residential basis) had been established at Wantage in 1859. In the early 1870s the Sisters of Nôtre Dame de Namur set up a similar centre (also residential) for pupil-teachers in their training college at Mount Pleasant in Liverpool. (No doubt this experiment encouraged the Liverpool School Board to start.) London and Liverpool were quickly copied by other large Boards. By the end of the nineteenth century the pupil-teacher centre had become the normal means of educating the urban pupil-teacher. In the rural areas it was not so easy; the motor-car had not yet by then even begun to revolutionize public transport. (It was, in fact, still not much more than a bad joke.)

It was largely by means of the pupil-teacher centre that the pupil-teacher was first emancipated, and then abolished. London and other School Boards progressively reduced his hours of teaching and increased those of study. In 1884 London put an end to the instruction of pupil-teachers before and after school, and introduced a 'half-time' system under which their pupil-teachers spent half the school week teaching and half at a pupil-teacher centre. From then on pupil-teacher centres (or the better among them) tended more and more to resemble secondary schools—as indeed many of them were to become during the early years of the twentieth century, when at long last England acquired a statutory system of secondary education. (Wales acquired hers a dozen years earlier, under the Welsh Intermediate Schools Act 1889.)

Gaps in the 1870 Act

The Elementary Education Act of 1870 undoubtedly filled the gaps it was designed to fill. The voluntary bodies which it recognized as partners in a State system, and the School Boards it created, between them covered the country with schools, not all of them good, but a surprising number much better than might have been expected. Thanks to this effort the principle of compulsory full-time education, explicitly stated in the 1870 Act, was translated into universal practice in the amazingly short space of ten years. Not universally effective practice, it is true; the task of persuading some parents to send their children to school proved a longer and stiffer one than providing the schools. But these parents were always a minority; the majority appreciated and supported the schools. With their assistance the teachers steadily raised the level of scholastic attainment. In 1882 it became necessary to add a seventh standard to the existing six. Even before this, enlightened School Boards—Leeds may have been the first in the field—were beginning to open 'Central' schools, later to be more generally called 'higher grade' schools, which offered more advanced studies to older and abler elementary school pupils. By the end of the century there were over a hundred higher grade schools, all giving in effect secondary education, though in many cases of a restricted character. Most of them accepted the generous grants offered by the Science and Art Department for its three-year course in Science—which unfortunately left little time for the humanities. Like the pupil-teacher centres, they were after the Education Act of 1902 quickly absorbed into the statutory system of secondary education.

In brief, the 1870 Act resulted in universal elementary education and at least the embryo of a secondary system; in higher levels of academic attainment; in a broadening of the elementary school curriculum; in greatly improved behaviour among the young, and in some cases among their parents and employers; and in a very considerable raising of the status of the teacher. The value of the positive

3

benefits it brought about can hardly be overestimated; but no appreciation of these should prevent a historian from pointing out that, being designed only to 'fill up gaps' in an extremely inadequate provision of elementary schools, the 1870 Act was itself not without gaps. Two of these have already been mentioned: that the Act did nothing statutorily to end, or hasten the end of, the infamous system of 'payment by results', and that it made no provision for recruiting and training the vastly increased number of teachers its successful implementation was bound to demand.

A third, most grievous, gap was the absence of any means for safe-guarding and improving children's health and well-being. The need for this seems apparently not to have been realized at the time; even Forster made no reference to it when introducing his Bill. It took years of economic depression, massive unemployment, widespread strikes, and warnings from medical men of the highest authority to wake the nation to the fact that schooling is of little avail to hungry or sick children. As the *Lancet* said in 1884, the educational system was not 'overworking children' (as had been alleged), but merely 'demonstrating that they are underfed'.[23]

Even then the Vice-President of the Committee of Council, Mr A. J. Mundella, did not consider official action necessary. He certainly encouraged school authorities to voluntary effort, pointing to the example set by the Devonshire village of Rousden, which had organized a scheme of cheap meals for hungry children; and he himself became president of a national voluntary society: The Central Council for Promoting Self-Supporting Penny Dinners. Voluntary effort took up the challenge, as well it might, for the report (made to the Education Department)[24] upon which the *Lancet* had commented had recorded instances of schools in which up to a third of the children were half-starved, and most lived mainly on bread and tea. Yet although subsequent reports and statements emphasized the desperate need of many thousands of children—as late as 1899 'an article in *Justice* claimed that nearly 500,000 children attended school hungry'[25]—it was not until 1906 that the State could be induced to act.

Thus again and again one is forced to realize the limitations of men's thought and feeling at any given point of time. During the first half of the nineteenth century devout Christians, deeply religious according to their lights, argued with all sincerity in favour of employing children of six, seven and eight in factories and workshops. In 1870 it was still thought proper to allow children under the age of ten to engage in 'gainful employment' for up to half the working day. And, as has been shown above, England's first Education Act did nothing to safeguard the health of children while they were at school —though in the north of England particularly the signs of ill-health, physical defect, and malnutrition were shockingly manifest in almost every street. Happily for England's future, voluntary effort, quickly supported by some at least of the large School Boards, pioneered in this field as it had in so many others; the names of George Lansbury, Will Thorne, Mrs H. M. Hyndman, Margaret McMillan, to select but four, and the organizations, chiefly working-class, which aided ailing and hungry children shed distinction upon the last quarter of the nineteenth century. Yet even they had ultimately to confess, as did their predecessors in the 1860s, that 'voluntary effort alone is not enough'; and England's acceptance of their verdict led to a sustained statutory effort which revolutionized children's health. That was not to come in the nineteenth century; but the twentieth quickly realized the necessity.

Notes

1. *Report of the Newcastle Commission*, vol. i, chap. 4, p. 243.
2. Hansard, clxxxviii, 15 July 1867, col. 1549. *Italics mine.*
3. Hansard, cxciv, 12 March, 1869, col. 1194.
4. *Return, confined to the Municipal Boroughs of Birmingham, Leeds, Liverpool and Manchester, of all Schools for the Poorer Classes of Children*, etc. H.C. No. 91, 1870.
5. Frank Smith. *A History of English Elementary Education 1760–1902*, University of London Press, 1931, p. 279.
6. T. Wemyss Reid. *Life of the Right Honourable William Edward Forster*, 3rd edn., 1886, vol. i, pp. 435–6.
7. *Ibid.*, pp. 441–2.
8. *Ibid.*, p. 446.
9. *Ibid.*, pp. 465–6.
10. Quoted from W. O. Lester Smith, *To Whom do Schools Belong?* 2nd edn., Blackwell, 1945, p. 87.
11. Reid, *Life of . . . Forster*, p. 464.
12. Hansard, cxcix, 17 February 1870, col. 440.
13. *Ibid.*, col. 441.
14. *Ibid.*, cols. 442–3.
15. *Ibid.*, col. 444.
16. *Ibid.*, col. 442.
17. *Ibid.*, col. 445. *Italics mine.*
18. Figures quoted from Marjorie Cruickshank. *Church and State in English Education, 1870 to the present day*, Macmillan, 1963, p. 190.
19. Lowe's Revised Code organized the elementary school into six 'standards', each with its examinable syllabus. Infants were not included, so the standards covered roughly the children aged between six and twelve.

20. *History of Elementary Education in England and Wales*, 3rd edn., University Tutorial Press, 1938, p. 123.
21. F. Smith. *A History of English Elementary Education* . . ., p. 295.
22. Figures from Committee of Council Annual Reports.
23. Quoted from W. H. G. Armytage. *Four Hundred Years of English Education*, Cambridge University Press 1964, p. 152.
24. *Report to the Education Department upon the alleged over-pressure of work in public elementary schools*, by Dr Crichton-Browne. Quoted from Brian Simon, *Education and the Labour Movement*, Lawrence & Wishart, 1965, pp. 133–4.
25. Simon, *op. cit.*, p. 134.

2

Widening Horizons

. . . the eighteen-seventies, perhaps the most seminal decade in our educational history . . .

Professor W. O. Lester Smith.[1]

In one most regrettable respect the 1870 Elementary Education Act was very much an isolated incident; it was concerned only with elementary education. It did nothing to bring this into any kind of relationship with any other branch of education. It did not even involve the training colleges, despite the fact that these existed solely for the purpose of preparing teachers for service in elementary schools. Viewed in the perspective of history, however, the Act falls into place as one of the most important—possibly *the* most important—of the educational experiments launched in a decade which saw a veritable galaxy of brilliant educational experiments.

Directly resulting from the Act (though occurring before this reached the Statute Book) was the foundation in June 1870 of the National Union of Elementary Teachers. This event meant infinitely more than the formation of a new professional association of teachers; it meant that the almost impossible had happened, that the existing teachers' associations—as sectarian as the societies which provided the schools—had at long last, after years of fratricidal dissension, agreed to sink their differences, and to act together in union on behalf of the profession to which they all belonged.

'The objects of the union are', said William Lawson, the first secretary, at the first conference, held on 10 September 1870:

to unite together, by means of local associations, public elementary teachers throughout the kingdom, in order to provide a machinery by means of which teachers may give expression to their opinions when occasion requires, and may also take united action in any matter affecting their interests.[2]

27

Inevitably, the Union had its domestic difficulties, some of them sectarian, during its earlier years. At times, too, its relations with the Education Department were strained, and for one agonizing period of six years non-existent; between 1884 and 1890 it was studiously ignored by the Department, which refused to recognize it as a negotiating body. Happily, this proved to be the 'darkest hour before the dawn'. Despite rebuffs the Union grew steadily in strength and influence under able and courageous leaders, outstanding among whom was T. E. Heller, secretary from 1873 to 1891. In 1889 it took the bold step of dropping the word 'elementary' from its title, thus by implication inviting all teachers, elementary, secondary, university, to join the all-embracing National Union of Teachers. [The response was not encouraging. Four secondary school associations were founded in the following three years: the Headmasters Association (1890), Assistant Masters, Headmasters of Private Schools, and Headmasters of Higher Grade and Organized Science Schools (1892).] The following year saw a new Permanent Secretary at the Education Department—and a completely new outlook. Sir George Kekewich promptly called the Union's officers into consultation, and made clear that he desired a friendly, but absolutely frank relationship.

Secondary schools for girls

If the lights turned to green for elementary education in 1870, for secondary they remained at amber. This is not to say that no advance was made, despite the disappointing inadequacy of the Endowed Schools Act of 1869, which proposed no pattern and provided no authority, central or local, for secondary education. But at least the Act made possible, through the redistribution of educational endowments, the filling of some gaps. One in particular deserves mention at length. Thanks to the initiative and persistence of a handful of determined women—Dorothea Beale, Frances Mary Buss, Anne Jemima Clough, Emily Davies, the two Shirreff sisters, Emily and Maria (Mrs Grey), Madame Bodichon, Miss E. C. Wolstenholme and others—the Schools Inquiry Commissioners (who had not been instructed even to consider the needs of girls) were made thoroughly aware, (i) that there was such a thing as girls' secondary education, (ii) that it was as important as boys', (iii) that most of it was abysmally bad, and therefore (iv) there was urgent need to reform it drastically, but that (v) this was next to impossible so long as endowments for it were virtually non-existent, and the schools had to be entirely self-supporting.

To the Commissioners' credit, they listened to the ladies. They even visited some girls' schools. They were shocked by much of what they saw. Female education, they recorded in their Report,[3] was characterized by 'want of thoroughness and foundation, want of system; slovenliness and showy superficiality; inattention to rudiments, undue time given to accomplishments, and those not taught intelligently or in any systematic manner . . .'

Parliament in its unwisdom ignored many of the wiser recommendations of the Schools Inquiry Commission. But in the Endowed Schools Act it did at least include the vague suggestion[4] that 'in framing schemes under this Act, provision shall be made as far as conveniently may be for extending to girls the benefits of endowments'. Not the most generous of wording. But the three Endowed School Commissioners appointed under the Act to rationalize and redistribute school endowments took their task seriously—so seriously indeed that they were accused of doing too much too quickly. They were replaced in 1874 by the Charity Commissioners. By the end of the century the Commissioners had brought into being over eighty endowed secondary schools for girls. Not a huge number—certainly not by comparison with the 900 new or revised schemes for boys' schools sanctioned during the same period. No wonder that the women, not content to await the slow processes of endowment, began themselves to establish schools. First in the field was Mrs Maria Grey, who in 1871 founded a 'National Union for the Education of Girls of all Classes above the Elementary', and in 1872 induced this Union to form a Girls' Public Day School Company.[5] Within five years the Company was running fourteen schools, within ten more than twenty, and before the end of the century nearly forty. The Church Schools Company, formed in 1883, though not exclusively devoted to girls' education gave much the greater part of its effort to this purpose; within a decade it had established twenty-four girls' schools, but only three (shortlived) boys' schools. Other bodies also set up girls' schools, but none on anything approaching the scale of these two companies.

What was even more remarkable than the actual foundation of so many girls' schools in so short a period of time was the intellectual standard they set and maintained. By 1880 the curricula of the GPDSC schools were ranging from Greek to gymnastics, from instrumental music to mathematics, and from political economy to physical science. And, their pupils were taking the same external examinations as boys —the Oxford and Cambridge Locals—and were getting as good results as their brothers, if not better.

There are still people who think that girls' secondary education took

29

the wrong turning in the 1870s, when the new 'high schools', following the example of Miss Buss's North London Collegiate School, deliberately set out to prove that girls could not only do the same academic subjects as boys but, measured by the same examinations, would achieve as high standards. As one early critic of this policy, who felt she had suffered from it, was later in life to write:[6]

> Instead of facing squarely the real needs of future wives and mothers, as the vast majority of girls were to be, Miss Buss seized the tempting instrument at her hand—the stimulus to mental ambition afforded by outside examinations. By this means the curriculum was ready-made. And thus, for better or worse, the education of girls became a feeble imitation of what the boys were doing, for the public examinations made no distinction of sex, and no woman's voice was heard at the examination boards.

About that *cri de coeur* three brief comments. First, many people would not agree that girls' secondary education in England and Wales has ever been since the days of Miss Beale and Miss Buss a 'feeble imitation of boys'. It has had its weaknesses—but so in all conscience has boys' education. Secondly, no person or body has yet offered a generally acceptable curriculum for girls which is fundamentally different from that for boys—and plenty of people, from the Consultative Committee of the Board of Education[7] to Sir John Newsom,[8] have attempted to do so. Thirdly, within a largely similar curricular pattern, the girls have carved out and consolidated areas of their own of special excellence. Not only in the distinctively women's subjects, the various branches of domestic science (or housecraft or home economics, whatever the currently fashionable title happens to be), but widely in the literary and aesthetic subjects, and, most interestingly, in physical education, in which as long ago as the 1880s a Swedish teacher of genius, Martina Bergman (later Madame Bergman Österberg), gave them a lead they have never lost.

While the competitive desire to show that girls were as able scholars as boys was probably the dominant idea in the minds of the heads of the new schools, it was not the only one. They genuinely wanted girls to have a really humane and liberal education; and the boys' schools and the universities offered the only models. Trusting to the 'faculty' psychology of the day, they believed that rigorously difficult subjects —especially Latin and Mathematics—were particularly valuable for training the mind. And, like all their fellow pioneers in the nineteenth century movement for women's emancipation, they ardently desired to fit women to earn an independent living, to kill the idea that marriage was the only career open to them, and that therefore the sole purpose of their education was to deck them out with 'accomplishments' designed to render them sexually more attractive to men.

This desire for economic emancipation illustrates the essentially middle-class outlook of the whole movement. Working-class women had always, since the earliest days of the Industrial Revolution, gone into paid employment—often to the exclusion of men.

A further reason why girls' secondary education was made so similar to that of boys may have been that almost all its outstanding advocates (who were also among its pioneer practitioners) had been given secondary and university education by men. Higher education for women had got off to a much earlier start than secondary education for girls. It began in a curiously personal way. The Reverend Frederick Denison Maurice, professor of history at King's College, London, had a sister working as a governess. He was therefore particularly interested in the foundation, in 1843, of the Governesses Benevolent Institution, which he and others formed to give financial assistance to members of that unprotected, underpaid, but overworked occupation if they fell on evil times—no infrequent occurrence, as was immediately made manifest; from the start the GBI was inundated with applications for aid. One of the principal reasons why so many British governesses were so wretchedly paid (and so often out of work) was that they had no professional qualifications—and no chance of securing any in Britain, because none existed. It was therefore suggested that the GBI should establish a system of examinations, and award teacher's diplomas comparable with those obtainable by governesses in Germany and Switzerland. The idea fell through because English governesses proved in general to be so ill-educated that they were unable to cope with the work demanded by professional syllabuses and examinations.

Higher education for women

Maurice was not to be beaten. He began to give lectures to women teachers. As the demand grew, he persuaded colleagues at King's College to assist him. Finally, in conjunction with the novelist Charles Kingsley and others, in 1848 he founded the Queen's College for Women and set it up in a house in Harley Street next door to the GBI.

Among the earliest students were Dorothea Beale and Frances Mary Buss. Although they were contemporaries, they apparently never met at the College, Miss Beale being a 'full-time day' student while Miss Buss, a teacher in her mother's school, was 'evening only'. Mrs Josephine Kamm, in her enchanting biography of these two eminent teachers,[9] records of Miss Buss that 'as there was no public transport available, she trudged night after night from Camden Town to Harley Street and back', six nights a week during her first term. Even for so tough a creature as Frances Mary this proved too much, so thereafter 'she compromised with four nights'.

Queen's College was established by Anglicans. Sectarian rivalry and, alas! discrimination, being rife in those days (and for long after), the nonconformists immediately felt that they must have their own college. Providentially, this was already to hand. A wealthy widow, Mrs Elizabeth Reid, acutely conscious of the defects of her own education, had for over a year been running classes in her home in Bedford Square which were similar to those at Queen's College. Seeing how successful the latter was proving, Mrs Reid was very willing to listen to suggestions that her classes should be established on a permanent basis, and provided with more accommodation. She put up the necessary money, and in 1849 the Bedford Square College for Women came into being. Though nominally managed by a Board of Governors, it remained essentially a private establishment until Mrs Reid's death in 1869. Then, fortified by the endowment she had left it, the College immediately applied for, and secured, a Royal Charter (as Queen's College had done sixteen years previously), and became affiliated with London University.

University extension lectures

While Bedford College was in process of securing its charter, exciting happenings of the utmost importance for the education of women were taking place farther north. They had their origin in the mind of a Liverpool woman who in the course of a varied life (most of her childhood was spent in the United States) had developed a passion for teaching: Anne Jemima Clough, sister of the poet Arthur Hugh Clough. As a teacher she gave evidence to the Schools Inquiry Commission in 1866. In this evidence (later published as a magazine article) she proposed the giving of series of lectures by distinguished professors to older pupils in secondary schools. If this scheme succeeded, she thought the idea might be enlarged: 'Lectures and instruction of a higher and more advanced character might be given, thus offering to the thoughtful of riper years, who had made good use of their early training, an opportunity of continuing their studies.'[10]

32

For a while Miss Clough's endeavours to realize this idea were discouragingly unsuccessful. But in 1867 the tide turned dramatically; addresses she gave interested Schoolmistresses' Associations in London and Manchester, and other teachers in Sheffield and Leeds. A fortunate letter to Trinity College, Cambridge, produced exactly the right lecturer, James Stuart, a newly elected Fellow of the College, who was very ready and willing to give such a series of lectures as Miss Clough desired. He rejected, however, the suggestion put forward by the north country associations of schoolmistresses that he should lecture on 'the theory and methods of teaching'—about which he knew nothing—and suggested instead a subject one would have thought as unacceptable to the associations as theirs was to him: the history of science. Happily, they agreed. Stuart gave his lectures during October and November to their audiences (largely secondary school mistresses and pupils) in Leeds, Liverpool, Manchester, and Sheffield. But he gave them also to other, very different audiences. Before he went north the Mechanics Institute at Crewe in Cheshire had approached him with a request that he would lecture there; when he did so in November the Institute faced him with an audience of 1500—mainly railwaymen—some three times as many as the women had mustered anywhere. A similar request had come from the famous Rochdale Equitable Pioneers Co-operative Society—the founding father of the Co-operative movement. Later, further requests came from Mechanics' Institutes at Nottingham, Derby and other places. Within a year or two Stuart was having to get other lecturers to help him.

In 1871, supported by petitions from the North of England Council for Promoting the Higher Education of Women (secretary, needless to say, Miss A. J. Clough), the Crewe Mechanics Institute, the Rochdale Pioneers, and the Mayor and citizens of Leeds, Stuart appealed to his University to take over the movement he had started. In 1873 Cambridge agreed—and 'university extension' was born. London followed in 1876, Oxford in 1878, and the Victoria University in 1886. Before the end of the century, hundreds of courses were being held all over the country, and nearly a dozen 'university extension colleges' had been established as permanent homes for extra-mural work. Of these colleges four—at Exeter, Nottingham, Reading, and Sheffield—were to be the foundations upon which full universities were later erected.

It was a historical accident that university extension began through an invitation from a body of women. Stuart had been actively contemplating some such project before he was approached by Miss Clough; her invitation merely gave him the opportunity to begin.

Once his lectures were a proved success (and that happened quickly, for he was an admirable lecturer), it became clear that his idea of a 'peripatetic university' could not be confined to women. Other historical accidents stamped upon university extension at least three of its most characteristic features. The story has often been told of how Stuart, being in a hurry to get away on one occasion from Rochdale, asked the hall-keeper if he could leave on the walls till the following week the diagrams with which he had been illustrating his lecture. Next week he found a group of his students waiting for him; they had been studying the diagrams, and wished to discuss them with him. Stuart was so impressed with the value of the time he spent with this group that he always thereafter added a discussion period to his lecture. What is possibly less well known is that the written work expected of students in university extension courses 'had its origin in the fact that it was considered improper for a young man such as Stuart to exchange oral question and answer with an audience of young ladies; to avoid this, written questions were circulated in advance and written answers were required'.[11] Nor, perhaps, do most people know of the close connection in these early days between university extension lectures and external examinations for women— and the row this caused.

When the University of Cambridge accepted responsibility for providing extra-mural courses it naturally appointed a Syndicate (with, equally naturally, Stuart as secretary) to do the actual work; that is, to approve schemes for courses, select lecturers, and set examinations. A perfectly normal academic procedure. But the examinations proposed—or one of them—produced for a time a large rift in the solidarity of the women's movement. Cambridge offered the North of England Council an examination exclusively for *women*. Such an implied suggestion of female inferiority infuriated Emily Davies (a northerner), who was an impassioned advocate of absolute equality for women. Ever since London University had, in 1862, refused to admit a woman—Elizabeth Garrett—to its matriculation examination, she had been campaigning unceasingly to secure for women the right to enter for *university* examinations. She had in 1865 scored a notable success when she persuaded the Cambridge Local Examinations Syndicate to admit girls to their examinations. In the same year she had sent to the Schools Inquiry Commission a memorial, signed by over 700 people,[12] pointing out that 'there are in England no public institutions for women analogous to the universities for men in which a complete education is given, and at the same time duly certified by an external body of recognized authority'.

Not only did Miss Davies and her 700 memorialists beg the Commission to pay 'special regard' to 'the need for such an institution'; Miss Davies and a few close friends set about creating one themselves. In October 1869 they took a house at Hitchin in Hertfordshire, and installed therein six young women, to read, first, the courses prescribed by Cambridge University for its Previous (i.e. entrance) examination, and, secondly, those leading to its first degree. In December 1870 they asked the University to admit five of their students to the Previous examination. The University proposed in reply a typically academic compromise; it would not formally admit women, but it would raise no objection to individual examiners allowing them to sit their papers. Miss Davies accepted the arrangement. Very soon her students began to demonstrate their quality (and by implication the intellectual ability of women); from 1872—the earliest possible date—they began to submit examination papers which, had they been written by men, would have secured them degrees—some of them very good degrees. (But, not being men, women had to wait until 1948 before Cambridge would give them real degrees. It is a curious paradox that the University which was the first in England to admit women to its degree examinations was the last to grant them degrees.)

What Emily Davies passionately desired was success in *degree* examinations, in *men's* examinations. The Hitchin prospectus made this perfectly clear:

> The Council [of the College] shall use such efforts as from time to time they may think most expedient and effectual to obtain for the students of the College admission to the examinations for the degrees of the University of Cambridge, and generally to place the College in connection with the University.[13]

Miss Clough, on the other hand, was willing to accept a purely women's examination. She was already in Cambridge when Miss Davies moved in 1873 to its outskirts and established her college at Girton, with herself as Principal. Miss Clough was also a 'Principal', but of a hall of residence, not a college. The purpose of the house in Regent Street which Professor Henry Sidgwick[14] opened in 1871 was to provide residential accommodation for women who wished to come to Cambridge to study, not for university degree examinations, but for the Cambridge Higher Local Examination, the exclusively women's examination which the University had set up in 1869.

But, predictably, the 'Association for promoting the Higher Education of Women in Cambridge' (originally the 'Lectures Association'), which the Regent Street hostel was designed to serve, did not long restrict its ambition to the Higher Local. In 1874, only two years after Girton presented its first students for a degree examination, the Association did the same; and of its two students who sat, one gained the equivalent of a near first-class degree, the other a second. In 1876 the hostel, after previous moves, settled at Newnham Hall, and there began its long climb to university college status.

Similar developments at Oxford began somewhat earlier but were slower to mature. In 1865 the Reverend Mark Pattison—most brilliant yet saddest of Oxford's nineteenth-century scholars—who was then Rector of Lincoln College, Oxford, with other dons started classes for girls (mainly from university teachers' families) who had left school but desired to continue their education. These classes petered out, but in 1873 a Ladies Committee (later to become the 'Association for the Education of Women') started others, with the idea of establishing and maintaining 'a system of instruction having general reference to the Oxford examinations'.[15] So widespread was the demand that, as at Cambridge, it was found necessary to provide hostels for women who lived at a distance. In 1879 two were opened: Somerville and Lady Margaret Hall. To complete the parallel with Cambridge, Lady Margaret Hall was, like Girton, an Anglican establishment, Somerville, like Newnham, undenominational.

Oxford and Cambridge were not unique in making a place for women; more generous provision was in fact being made by London. This University admitted girls to its Local Examinations in 1870, created for them in 1875 a Higher Local Examination, and in 1878 became the first university in Britain to make its degrees available to women. Two residential colleges for women were established within a few years: Westfield in 1882, and the Royal Holloway in 1886. The latter was originally intended by its founder, the pill maker Thomas Holloway, to be a women's university.

Rise of Redbrick

London was the first English university to admit women students on terms of equality with men; it was not, however, the first university institution to do so. That honour belongs, paradoxically, to Owens College, Manchester. Paradoxically, because John Owens, its founder, had in his will denied women any share in the college he endowed; this was to provide means of educating 'young persons of the male sex' only. But in 1871, when the College was formally incorporated by Act of Parliament, this unfortunate limitation was removed; and Owens College became in respect of its admission policy, as in so many other respects, the exemplar for the completely new type of English university that was to grow up during the latter part of the nineteenth century and the first few decades of the twentieth: the 'civic' university, or 'Redbrick' as it was in 1943 affectionately labelled by the pseudonymous 'Bruce Truscot' (the late Professor E. Allison Peers), himself a Redbrick professor.

London ought, of course, to have had the first Redbrick; the 'godless institution in Gower Street' (now University College London) was established in the 1820s to uphold the two principles on which all the later Redbrick colleges were to be based: university education at modest cost, and 'irrespective of class or creed'. But sectarian bigotry—the prime bane of English education throughout the nineteenth century—threw up at once a competing denominational college, the Anglican King's College, prevented the two colleges from agreeing a common constitution, and left London University until 1900 a mere skeleton of a university: an examining body with no teaching function.

Yet by one of the happiest of historical accidents—or should it rather be regarded as an outstanding example of the English genius for improvisation?—this emasculated London University was to prove of inestimable benefit to all the Redbrick colleges, to numerous other university colleges in the British Commonwealth and Empire, and to millions of private students (of whom I am proud to have been one) all over the world. In 1858 the University, overwhelmed with applications from establishments wishing to affiliate to it, cut the Gordian knot by throwing open its degrees to all persons, anywhere, who could pass its examinations. It was by preparing students for London University's 'external' degrees that every English university college for close on a century proved its right to full university status. (The last was Leicester, in 1957.) To the present day colleges in emergent countries are being similarly assisted by London. And the stream of external students working in colleges of further education, or with correspondence colleges, or on their own, shows no sign of diminishing.

As London could not claim to possess a real university, the distinction of having the first 'Redbrick' fell to Manchester. But this distinction had for some years to be shared with two other northern cities, Leeds and Liverpool. In 1880 Her Majesty Queen Victoria granted a Royal Charter, not to the University of Manchester for which Owens College had petitioned, but to a federal Victoria University in which a number of colleges could be incorporated. This was the compromise that ended, for the time being, a difficult and unhappy situation, caused by intercity rivalry, which had led Leeds, Liverpool and a dozen other towns to petition the Privy Council *not* to grant a University to Manchester. Manchester had, however, the consolation that the Victoria University was to be located in that city, and that its first constituent college was to be the 100 per cent Mancunian Owens College, now almost thirty years old, and served by distinguished scholars who had established for it a national—and even international —reputation in the world of learning.

In view of the pioneer role that Owens College played in the creation of the modern English university, it is a sobering thought that the money which founded it might (according to several authorities) have gone quite another way; in short, might have been left by John Owens to his closest personal friend, George Faulkner. There are different versions of the story. The following is that given by Edward Fiddes, a former registrar of the University.[16]

> One day Owens called on Faulkner and informed him that he had left him all he had. Faulkner refused to accept the bequest on the ground that he had enough already. The difference of opinion ended in a tiff which lasted for a week when Owens again called on Faulkner and urged Faulkner to agree, as he himself had no near relation. Faulkner again refused and persuaded Owens to use his money for the establishment of a college in Manchester, reminding him of his strong objection to the Tests [i.e. the religious tests imposed at Oxford, Cambridge and Durham Universities].

> So John Owens's £96,000 went to found in his native city 'an institution for providing or aiding the means of instructing and improving young persons of the male sex (and being of an age not less than fourteen years) in such branches of learning and science as are now and may be hereafter usually taught in the English Universities . . .'

The bequest was subject to the observance of 'two fundamental and immutable rules and conditions', of which one was that if there were more applicants than the college could cope with preference was to be given, first, to inhabitants of Manchester, and secondly of South Lancashire. The other, and crucial, condition was that:

> the students, professors, teachers, and other officers and persons connected with the said institution, shall not be required to make any declaration as to, or submit to any test whatsoever of, their religious opinions, and that nothing shall be introduced in the matter or mode of education or instruction in reference to any

religious or theological subject which shall be reasonably offensive
to the conscience of any student, or of his relations, guardians, or
friends, under whose immediate care he shall be.[17]

In prohibiting religious tests Owens followed the precedent set nearly
twenty years previously by the founders of University College,
London—though he did not go so far as they did, and prohibit any
religious education. Within not much more than another twenty
years religious tests were to be prohibited in all English universities.

Owens College was not only the first of its kind; it remained unique
for twenty years. Or almost unique. At the other end of the country, in
Southampton, a second university was struggling (but much less
successfully) to be born. In 1850, a year before Owens College opened,
'an eccentric recluse', Henry Robinson Hartley, died leaving to *his*
native city (which he had only rarely and briefly visited during the
previous quarter of a century) a sum slightly larger even than that left
by John Owens to Manchester. Hartley's intentions seem to have been
vaguely similar to those of Owens, but unfortunately his expression of
them was diffuse and obscure. He desired the Corporation of Southampton, to which he left nearly £103,000, to provide for 'The study
and advancement of the sciences of Natural History, Astronomy,
Antiquities, Classical and Oriental Literature in the town ... by
[such means as] forming a Public Library, Botanic Gardens, Obser-
vatory, and collections of objects in connection with the above
sciences'.[18] Not altogether surprisingly, his relatives contested the
will. An eight years' lawsuit ensued which reduced Hartley's bequest
to under £43,000—considerably less than half the original amount.

Then there arose a second cause for dispute. Hartley's will had
made no specific reference to a college or to any other *teaching* establishment. But many Southampton people believed that this was what
Hartley had intended. Finally, to cut a very long controversy short, a
'Hartley Institution', comprising a lecture hall, museum, library,
reading room and classrooms, was opened in October 1862. At the
time the total staff was a 'Librarian-cum-Curator' (later to be called
'Principal') and a porter. Forty years were to elapse before the Institution, which had even more than the normal run of troubles during
those years, was incorporated as a university college, and ninety
before it became a university.

In the 1870s colleges intended to offer courses at university level
came into being almost every year. The causes of their foundation
were various, but prominent among them was the anxiety felt by
politicians, industrialists, educationists and other informed members

4

of the public about the decreasing competitiveness of British goods in the rapidly expanding markets of the world. Not only the educationists suspected that, in part at any rate, this loss of the paramountcy Britain had earlier enjoyed was due to the efficient systems of scientific and technological education which had been built up by the more aggressive of its European competitors—Austria, Belgium, France, Prussia, and Switzerland in particular—and the almost complete lack of any such system, or indeed of such education, in Britain.

Welsh aspirations realized

But the first of the new colleges to be founded was born out of broader and deeper desire. Welshmen had for centuries dreamed of a University of Wales—or more than one. Way back in the early years of the fifteenth century Owen Glendower, patriot and nationalist, had proposed two, one in the north and the other in the south of the Principality. Nothing came of his proposal—not altogether surprisingly, seeing that he made it to the King of France, as an item in a treaty of alliance against the King of England. The dream never completely faded, but over four and a half centuries were to elapse before it was transformed into a reality. Then, in 1867, after a dozen years or more of discussion and fund-raising, Mr (later Sir) Hugh Owen and the other idealists he had gathered round him, purchased for £10,000 a bankrupt railway hotel in Aberystwyth. Two sites for a university college had previously been offered, one in the north, near Bangor, and one in the south, near Llantwit Major in Glamorgan; but money was short, and appeared likely to remain so, and the Castle Hotel at Aberystwyth seemed much too good a bargain to be missed. Even so, it was five years before the University College of Wales could be opened; and even then more than three-quarters of the purchase price was still owing. For over a decade the College existed on the edge of bankruptcy. 'In 1879 the college had a balance at the bank of only £319. In a desperate effort to economize, among other measures it dropped its Professor of Music—in Wales of all countries!'[19] Aberystwyth was kept going by the tenacity of Hugh Owen and the pennies of the people of Wales. Between 1863 and 1880 Owen raised over £65,000 by public appeals; to this amount, he himself estimated, at least 100,000 people had made contributions of under half a crown.

During this period more than one unsuccessful attempt was made to secure a subsidy for the struggling college from the British Government, which, though at all times extremely reluctant to give such aid, had made grants to the Scottish universities ever since the union of the

Kingdoms in 1707, and to London from its foundation. In 1880 a letter from Owen touched the heart of Mr Gladstone, who had recently become, for the second time, Prime Minister. Gladstone set up a Departmental Committee, with as Chairman the first Lord Aberdare, at that time probably the most influential man politically in Wales. The Committee's terms of reference were:

To inquire into the present condition of Intermediate [i.e. secondary] and Higher Education in Wales, and to recommend the measures which they may think advisable for improving and supplementing the provision that is now, or might be made, available for such education in the Principality.

The Committee's Report, issued in 1881, brought reforms of the utmost importance in Welsh secondary and university education. Those in secondary education were unfortunately delayed for eight years; nevertheless, the passing in 1889 of the Welsh Intermediate Education Act gave Wales a statutory system of secondary education nearly a decade and a half before England. Advance in university education came much more quickly. The Aberdare Committee had found everywhere a desire for two university colleges in Wales—as always, for one in the north and one in the south. So strong was this desire that the continued existence of the University College of Wales, at any rate in Aberystwyth, was for a while at risk; the Committee's Report actually suggested that it might be moved either to Bangor or Caernarvon. The British Government, however, decided to keep it at Aberystwyth, and to found another two colleges, at Bangor and Cardiff. Moreover, it made the crucial decision to give each college an annual grant of £4,000. So promptly was this decision carried into effect that Aberystwyth received its first grant in 1882. The following year the University College of South Wales and Monmouthshire opened, in Cardiff, and in 1884 the University College of North Wales, at Bangor. (The latter, like Aberystwyth, began its life in a hotel.) Within ten years the three colleges were united in a federal University of Wales. The only sad note in this success story is that the theological college of St David's at Lampeter in Cardiganshire, though much the oldest institution of higher education in Wales (it was founded in 1822), and empowered to award degrees in divinity and arts, was unable, for denominational reasons, to consider becoming a member of the federation.

The Government grants which ensured the future of the Welsh university colleges were not extended to those in England until 1889, by which time some of the latter were financially almost at the end of their tether. This was partly because of the failure of benefactors, whether individuals or corporate bodies, to realize that it is far more costly to maintain than to found a teaching establishment, and partly because, as Sir James Mountford, one time Vice-Chancellor of the University of Liverpool, has put it in his admirable book on the British Universities: 'Whatever the first expectations may have been, students did not flock to enter the new portals of learning, and in many colleges even the small number of students fluctuated up and down in a disconcerting way.'[20] The principal reason for this, as was to become increasingly evident during the last quarter of the nineteenth century, was the absence of any organized system of secondary education.

Of foundations there was, as already implied, a veritable spate during the 1870s and the early 1880s. In 1871 industrialists largely financed the founding in Newcastle-upon-Tyne of a College of Physical Science, affiliated to the University of Durham (as strange a marriage as ever was). In 1872 industrialists in Leeds, stirred to action by 'a trade depression and competition from the Continent',[21] drew up plans for a Yorkshire college of science; and this, thanks to generous gifts from the Clothworkers' Livery Company, was opened in 1874. In 1876 a strange combination of enthusiasts founded in Bristol a college of science for the West of England: they included John Percival, headmaster of the recently established proprietary school at Clifton (now Clifton College); Benjamin Jowett, the famous Master of Balliol College, Oxford; the ancient trade association of the Bristol Merchant Venturers, the civic authorities, and the thirty-year-old medical school.

A year later the Nottingham City Council made history by founding the first municipal university college in England (though not in Britain; the Edinburgh Corporation did the same three centuries earlier). The Nottingham civic authorities were, it is true, prompted by an anonymous benefactor who offered £10,000 to provide a permanent home for university extension lectures given in the town. But they reacted generously and imaginatively. They had already accepted responsibility for, and housed, but only in temporary buildings, a free library, and a natural history museum belonging to the Mechanics Institute. Why not, argued the Council, supplement the anonymous donor's gift, and erect a building that would be large enough for all three purposes? And so it was agreed. Despite noisy complaints from some of their ratepayers the Council voted a capital sum of £100,000 and, most prudently, allocated the product of a three-halfpenny rate for the maintenance of the new institution.

When the building was opened, in 1881, it was described as a 'University college'—but the town had to wait twenty-two years for a Royal Charter confirming this title. The Privy Council could not stomach the idea of a university institution governed by a town council.

Individual industrialists led the way at Sheffield and Birmingham. At Sheffield, Mark Firth, a steel manufacturer, as Mayor of the town in 1874–5 helped to organize a series of university extension lectures which proved extremely successful. Like the anonymous Nottingham donor, Firth was greatly impressed; and there were not wanting friends, including A. J. Mundella, the M.P. for Sheffield, ready to suggest that this might well be the beginning of a University of Sheffield. The upshot was that:

> Whereas the said Mark Firth, being convinced of the benefits resulting from the lectures and classes held in Sheffield . . . and being desirous of aiding to carry out in his native town of Sheffield aforesaid a system of higher education in connection with the English Universities, for the promotion of the moral, social and intellectual elevation of his fellow townsmen, is desirous of providing, at his sole expense, a building . . . to be for ever used and employed for the benefit of the inhabitants of the said town of Sheffield and others, for such purposes of higher education, and especially for the teaching and cultivation of any branches of learning taught or cultivated in the English Universities.[22]

At Birmingham, Josiah Mason, a selfmade man of many trades, was moved by very different considerations. His aim was industrial efficiency of the highest order; and he knew exactly the type of institution that would produce it. Rejecting any idea of putting his money into an existing establishment, and being determined not to court failure by financial cheese-paring, he surpassed the generosity of all other benefactors up to that time by giving (in 1870) the princely sum of £200,000 to found a college of science that would serve the Midlands by providing, 'upon terms which render it easily available by persons of all classes . . . thorough systematic education and instruction adapted to the practical, mechanical, and artistic requirements of the manufactures and industrial pursuits of the Midland District . . . to the exclusion of mere literary education and instruction, and of all teaching of theology'.[23] In other words, the Mason Science College was to be a technical college in the strictest sense of the term. Happily, Mason was persuaded, before it was too late, of the worldly unwisdom of this; if the original constitution stood, he was told, the college would have little chance either of being recognized by any university or of becoming itself a full university, or even a constituent college in a federal university. The Mason Science College opened in 1880; in the following year its founder added to its trust deed a supplement permitting the teaching of Greek and Latin and 'such a course of study as shall qualify for degrees in arts and science in the Victoria University or the London University or any other university of which the institution shall form part'.

Federal university

The Victoria University, founded in the same year as Mason College opened, was a new phenomenon in English education: a federal university with full teaching powers. It was born out of the ambition—and subsequent frustration—of Owens College, Manchester. That enterprising venture, once it had proved its capacity to survive—and this it had done before 1870, despite the refusal of the British Government to grant-aid it—set its course full steam ahead for university status. It 'devised a new constitution in 1871, opened its new buildings in 1873, began to admit women in 1874, and proposed to become a university in 1875'.[24] This forward march was abruptly halted shortly after the College petitioned for a university charter, by a counter petition *against* a Manchester University, presented by the Corporations of Leeds, Liverpool and a dozen other towns. Prolonged negotiations between Manchester, Leeds and Liverpool resulted in an agreement that a university should be located in Manchester, but that it should be a federal university. Owens College would be its first constituent member; the Yorkshire College (which dropped the words 'of Science' from its title in 1878) would join as soon as it could, and a college still to be born at Liverpool would make up the envisaged trinity of members. The Privy Council, which had taken a lot of persuading to grant a Charter at all, refused to allow the name of Manchester to appear in the University's title. Happily, the Queen was more graciously forthcoming. The Victoria University finally came into being (much behind schedule) in 1880.

By this time the Liverpool civic authorities, with the support of their citizens, were well ahead with their plans. They had the good sense to apply for a Royal Charter constituting their proposed foundation from the start a university college. The Charter was granted in 1881, and offset to some extent the insufficient financial resources and the inadequate building—a disused lunatic asylum—with which the College opened in 1882. Affiliation with the Victoria University followed in 1884, and in the same year the College absorbed the old-established Medical School attached to the Royal Infirmary. At Leeds matters had not gone nearly so smoothly; local support for the Yorkshire College of Science had been conspicuously meagre. But in 1884 this College also acquired an old-established medical school; and three years later was accepted into the Victoria University.

Unhappily, it has to be recorded that England's first attempt at a federal university did not prove a success. There was never very much chance that it would. All university business was done at Manchester —which provoked dark feelings of inferiority in the other partners, who anyhow objected to having to travel all that way to Senate or Council. When Birmingham, having turned down the idea of affiliating to Victoria, got its own Charter in 1900 the federation quickly broke up. It has been left to Wales and London to demonstrate that (despite formidable distances between colleges) federation at university level is not impossible. Both Universities have had periods when the federal structure was threatened, but in both it has survived.

The nineteenth-century university colleges opened an entirely new era in English (and Welsh) higher education. That is clear today, when Redbrick—rather than any other form—is the typical English university. So it is salutary to recall how easily any or all of these colleges might have been sunk without trace during their novitiate. For many years they were, almost without exception, financially below subsistence level, even after the State began, very modestly, in 1889 to grant-aid them. The numbers of their students remained embarrassingly small, of full-time students doing work of degree standard insignificant. Even towards the end of the century, when several of them were on the point of achieving full university status, the majority of the students in most of these university colleges were evening students, many of them doing work not much, if any, above the level of today's Certificate of Secondary Education.

Technical education

Three factors in particular were gradually to give them standards, stability, and strength: the considerable number of distinguished scholars who risked their academic careers to come and serve in them—H. E. Roscoe at Manchester, W. M. Hicks at Sheffield, Viriamu Jones at Cardiff, for example; the annual grants the Government was induced to make them from 1889 onwards; and the opportunity given them by the Government in 1890 to undertake the training of teachers. But until the final decade of the nineteenth

45

century theirs was in the main a story of courageous improvisation. Financially, and often perhaps academically, they were less viable than the three institutions for scientific and technological education that were established in London during the 1870s and 1880s, largely with money contributed (not always over-willingly) by the immensely wealthy Livery Companies: the City and Guilds of London Institute (1878), the Finsbury Technical College (1883), and the Central Technical College at South Kensington (1884). The second and third of these resulted from the foundation of the first, which was designed (*inter alia*), (i) to grant-aid existing establishments giving technical education, and (ii) to set up and maintain 'model' technical colleges in London. Finsbury and South Kensington were 'models'. The Finsbury College was to train, by means of evening classes, boys and men for subordinate positions of responsibility in industry, South Kensington the professional grades—engineers, architects, works managers, and teachers of technical subjects. (Despite strenuous efforts by Thomas Henry Huxley, a founder member of the College Council, it never did much of the last.)

With but a slight twist of fortune this movement might have produced England's first technological university. This was what the 'City and Guilds' was originally intended to be, and what its first Director, Philip Magnus, and many others later hoped the Central College might become. Circumstances decided otherwise; though the Central College eventually acquired university status (and that after a shorter period of time than some of the provincial colleges), it was as a constituent member of the Imperial College of Science and Technology (founded in 1907), itself one of the 'Schools' of the recently reconstituted University of London.

A movement comparable in some respects, but with a much stronger social flavour—'an English blend of philanthropy, adult education, and technical instruction', as Michael Argles has delightfully labelled it[25]—was that which began when Quintin Hogg in 1882 bought the bankrupt Polytechnic in Regent Street—originally an exhibition hall of scientific marvels—and turned it into a night school and social centre. After a somewhat shaky start the 'Regent Street Poly' became such a success that other polytechnics were soon projected. The Drapers and the Goldsmiths among the London Livery Companies became keenly, and generously, interested; as the presentday Queen Mary and Goldsmiths' Colleges of the University of London bear witness. But what really caused a boom in polytechnics was an Act of Parliament passed in 1883, the City Parochial Charities Act. This diverted to up-to-date purposes charity funds in over 100 London parishes which had outgrown their usefulness. The Commissioners appointed under the Act offered London £1 million from these funds to found more polytechnics, provided voluntary effort matched £ for £. Within the following twenty years ten polytechnics had been established and endowed. All, except the Goldsmiths' Institute (later College), worked according to schemes prepared by the Charity Commissioners, and so, though they varied greatly in details, they manifested a family resemblance, typified by a combination of advanced academic and vocational studies, technical and trade courses, and firstrate social and recreative facilities, indoor and out.

Up to 1890 all the various bits and pieces of the educational service —elementary, secondary, technical, teacher training, university— functioned very largely in isolation from one another. The 'public' and some of the endowed grammar schools had more or less intimate links with Oxford or Cambridge colleges, through closed scholarships or personal contacts. A wide variety of establishments preparing students for the external degrees of London University was linked, at least by letter, with that austere examining body. An even wider variety of establishments was linked with the Science and Art Department of the Committee of Council ('South Kensington'), since this body ladled out grants for science courses and examinations with a fine impartiality to all comers: elementary schools, secondary schools, 'night schools', pupil-teacher centres, technical colleges, mechanics institutes, training colleges, university colleges, universities.

But all these were links between individual institutions; between the various parts of the educational service there was neither constitutional nor organic connection. Elementary education, secondary education, technical instruction, extra-mural adult education, university education: each functioned as a separate 'system', isolated from the others, and kept apart, unhappily, by social rather than educational barriers. Of these, the system of elementary education (the only one that was, in fact, systematized) was the most completely isolated. Yet interestingly enough, it was to be intimately involved in the first big move towards a more coordinated service.

Coordination begins

This took place in 1890. It did not, of course, just come out of the blue; a long series of apparently disconnected events had for decades been leading up to it. There is always an element of risk in naming an exact date as marking the start of an educational movement or process; but, accepting that risk, it may be suggested that 1870 started two important trends towards coordination. First, the passing of the Elementary Education Act made possible a large expansion of this part of the country's educational service, and consequently required for it more (and better trained) teachers. The appointment in the same year of the Devonshire Commission on Scientific Instruction and the Advancement of Science had no obvious or immediate relevance to the passing of the Elementary Education Act. Its connection with this Act lay partly in the fact that it helped to stimulate the foundation of provincial university colleges, which only twenty years later were to become the main agencies for training more teachers for elementary schools.

The Devonshire Commission led also to the Royal Commission on Technical Instruction and that in turn to the Technical Instruction Act of 1889, which not only systematized a second branch of the educational service, but also brought into the administration of public education the all-purpose local authorities newly created by the Local Government Act of 1888: the County Councils and County Borough Councils. Without such local authorities a genuinely coordinated system of public education could never have been brought about. The incessant warfare between London's School and Technical Education Boards is ample evidence of that.

While the Local Government Bill was going through Parliament, another Royal Commission, the Cross Commission on the working of the Elementary Education Acts in England and Wales, was formulating the recommendation which led to universities and university colleges being allowed to establish 'day training colleges' for the express purpose of training teachers for public elementary schools; and thus to the first organic link between elementary and university education.

Among the strongest forces making for coordination were the growing overlap between the work done by elementary, secondary, and technical schools, and the plethora of central authorities which not only made such overlapping possible, but positively fostered it. As has been noted, very shortly after the passing of the 1870 Act some of the larger School Boards began to establish 'central', or 'higher grade', schools for senior pupils desiring more than the normal elementary school curriculum, and pupil-teacher centres for the general education of their prospective teachers. Both types of institution gave, ncreasingly, what was in fact secondary education; and for many years the Education Department more or less openly connived at this, while the Science and Art Department gave it large support by means of not ungenerous grants. In 1889 the Technical Instruction Act extended the overlap by bringing secondary education, so to speak, under the wing of technical, in that: 'It permitted county councils to spend money not merely on technical education in the strict sense, that is, direct preparation for a specific occupation, but on such general education as was necessary to enable the pupil to profit by a true technical course.'[26] This became extremely important when, in 1890, the county councils acquired a huge (and completely unanticipated) annual windfall: the so-called 'whiskey money'. A proposal in Parliament that the proceeds of a tax on spirits should be largely expended in compensating publicans dispossessed of their licences was strongly contested, among others by Sir William Mather, joint founder of the engineering firm of Mather and Platt, and one of the pioneers of part-time day release. He argued that the money ought to be put to much better uses, for example, to subsidize technical education, an urgent national need. And to that use it was put (or most of it), and a handsome fortune it proved; during the following ten years (it was discontinued after the 1902 Education Act) it brought in annually amounts that rose from just under half-a-million pounds to well over three-quarters of a million. (How valuable it was may be judged from the fact that it produced for 'technical education' about ten times as much money as the councils drew from the rates for that purpose.) More than any other single factor, the 'whiskey money' put technical education on the local authority map during the 1890s.

Meanwhile, the recommendation of the Cross Commission concerning day training colleges was also (though indirectly) adding to the possibilities of overlap. The task of this Commission, according to its terms of reference, was 'to inquire into the working of the Elementary Education Acts, England and Wales'. Its main business was to discover how well (or badly) the voluntary schools were faring under those Acts. As part of a general scrutiny the Commission was bound to look at the training and supply of teachers; and as the supply was known to be inadequate and the training strongly suspected by many people to be unsatisfactory, the Commission had been asked to scrutinize both matters thoroughly. In the course of this scrutiny it was to investigate the possibility of establishing in England and Wales nonresidential day training colleges, such as there were in Scotland.

Pressure to make this particular investigation had come principally from the larger School Boards. They wanted more trained teachers, they wanted them better trained, and, their areas being as a rule strongholds of nonconformity, they did *not* want them trained in denominational colleges under the aegis of the Church of England. The School Boards (and the nonconformists) had a very real grievance; the total annual output of trained teachers was much too small; all the training was in the hands of voluntary colleges, more than three-quarters of them denominational colleges—in which it was exceedingly difficult, and in most cases impossible, for anyone not belonging to the particular denomination to obtain a place. Admittedly, large numbers of the teachers trained in these colleges took posts in Board schools (because of the better salaries and working conditions), but their training had left its imprint on them, and it was not the imprint the Boards desired.

Day training colleges

The Cross Commission, after listening to much confusing opinion—many witnesses, for example, among them specialist HMIs, seemed to regard residence as the only means of safeguarding the morals of prospective teachers—was not surprisingly of two minds about the matter, as it was about many others. The majority advocated a limited experiment with day training colleges. The Government accepted this advice; but it refused to allow School Boards to run any of the colleges, despite their willingness, and obvious ability, to do so—the Birmingham Board had put up as good a scheme as anyone. Universities and university colleges only were to be permitted to undertake so risky an experiment.

The university institutions, especially the struggling university colleges, leapt at the chance; as well they might, since it promised a regular supply of financially reliable students—grant-aided Queen's scholars—and so a welcome addition to university or college funds. Six university training departments were established in 1890, one by the University of Durham, at Newcastle, and five by university colleges. Four more departments were set up in each of 1891 and 1892. By 1900 there were sixteen, containing nearly 1200 students, and producing nearly one-quarter of the annual output of trained teachers for public elementary schools. Such an increase in supply was immensely helpful to the schools, though it did not by any means satisfy their demands—if only because as supply increased staffing standards rose. But the consequences, both immediate and long-term, of the decision by the university authorities to undertake the training of teachers were more important and far reaching than any boost to the supply of teachers, however substantial, could by itself have been. Seven deserve particular mention.

First, the hitherto complete isolation of the public elementary school from higher education was ended. Henceforth, on the one hand, a considerable proportion of the teachers entering elementary schools had been educated in university institutions, and on the other, university teachers had learned to know, and usually to respect, this new stratum of the student population; they found its intellectual ability generally good, and its capacity for hard work almost invariably so. Secondly, the near monopoly of teacher training which the religious denominations had enjoyed ever since training colleges in the modern sense had begun was also ended. Thirdly, the widely held conviction that institutional life was an essential element in the training of a teacher was successfully challenged. Fourthly, the public elementary school benefited from receiving more highly educated and more socially sophisticated teachers. Many of the day training college students obtained university degrees along with their teacher's certificate, and all were taught academic subjects by university teachers, usually—though not always—in classes containing students from other walks of life and destined for other careers. All could share with these students the social and recreational amenities of their university or university college. Fifthly, something approaching academic respectability was conferred upon the subjects 'education' and 'educational psychology' when they were taught by university teachers of distinction who were capable of transforming these inchoate aggregations of doctrine and folklore into ordered disciplines of university calibre.

Sixthly, before long the new colleges began to train teachers for secondary schools, until then only undertaken (with rare exceptions) by a few pioneering women's colleges and girls' schools. By 1900 almost all the day training colleges had secondary departments as well as elementary. It is sad to have to record that, after a promising start, when it looked as though the two groups would train happily together, this bifurcation proved disastrously divisive. There had always been a great gulf between elementary and secondary school teachers; but this had derived from differences of social class. The development by the university institutions of secondary training departments (which within twenty years ousted the elementary departments) divided teachers who came from the same social environment.

Seventhly, the establishment of day training colleges quite simply kept alive the Faculties of Arts in most of the university colleges.

A liberal code

Another event which made the year 1890 memorable was the Code of Regulations for Public Elementary Schools with which Sir George Kekewich signalled his accession to the post of Permanent Secretary of the Education Department. At first sight it might seem that the publication of this Code was completely unrelated to the other events occurring about this time. Actually there was a close connection, both in the general sense that it introduced a more liberal conception of the function of the elementary school, and thereby made coordination with other branches of the educational service potentially easier; and more particularly in that most of the happier articles in the Code reflected recommendations made by the Cross Commission. (It cannot be accepted that the reforms of the 1890 Code were entirely due to Kekewich, however much his delightful but somewhat vainglorious autobiography[27] may imply it. But all credit to him for entering fully into the spirit of the recommendations, for bringing into the work of the Department a quite new concern for the wellbeing of children, and for transforming the relationship between the Department and the teachers' professional associations.)

The 1890 Code had outstanding merits. It went a long way towards ending the vicious system of 'payment by results'. The grants for individual passes at HMI's annual examination in the '3 Rs' were at last abolished—after twenty-seven years in which they had progressively poisoned relations between teachers and inspectors and, much worse, between teachers and children. They were replaced by a fixed 'principal' grant based on examination of a sample of the pupils—and even this modicum of examining was progressively discarded between 1893 and 1897.

These changes closed a despicable era in English elementary education. What gave hope for the future were the principles on which the 1890 Code was based. In Sir George Kekewich's words:[28]

> The Code was based, as far as the actual teaching of the children was concerned, on two main principles. The first was to substitute for the bald teaching of facts, and the cramming which was then necessary in order that the children might pass the annual examination and earn the grant, the development of interest and intelligence and the acquirement of real substantial knowledge. . . . The second main principle of the Code was the recognition for the first time of the duty of the State to care for the physical welfare of the children, and to make physical culture an integral part of their

school life. Physical education, sports and games, out-of-door teaching in fresh air, were therefore encouraged.

A single central authority

To bring about a thoroughgoing coordination of public education in England two large administrative reforms had to be effected. There had to be one single authority for education, both at the centre and in the localities, and there had to be an organized system of secondary education. The lack of both had been deplored for half a century, but all endeavours to provide them had failed—the last being an attempt in 1892 to introduce legislation enabling the county councils to administer secondary education. During the next year bodies as varied as the Independent Labour Party, meeting at Bradford, and representatives of secondary education, meeting at Oxford under the chairmanship of the Vice-Chancellor of the University, called upon the Government to take action. In March 1894 the Queen, on the advice of Lord Rosebery's Liberal Government, appointed a Royal Commission, under the chairmanship of Mr James (later Viscount) Bryce:

> To consider what are the best methods of establishing a well-organized system of secondary education in England, taking into account existing deficiencies and having regard to such local sources of revenue for endowments or otherwise as are available or may be made available for this purpose and to make recommendations accordingly.

It was a well chosen body of Commissioners. It even included three women—the first ever to sit on a Royal Commission: Dr Sophie Bryant, Lady Frederick Cavendish, and Mrs E. M. Sidgwick. It worked speedily, and produced within seventeen months a Report which is a landmark in English educational history. Appointed, as its terms of reference indicate, to remedy one of the two major educational defects which afflicted the country, it pointed the way towards remedying both. Its two principal recommendations were:

> 1. The establishment of a single central authority for secondary education, headed by a Minister of Education. This authority, which should take over the Education Department, the Science and Art Department, and the educational functions of the Charity Commission, should also be the central authority for elementary education.

53

2. The establishment of local authorities for all types of secondary education, including higher grade and organized science schools. A majority of the members of these authorities should be chosen by the county councils (in the county boroughs equal numbers by the council and the School Board), and the authorities should be given wide powers to 'supply, maintain, and aid schools' out of the rates.

Seven years were to elapse before the second of those recommendations was translated (in much modified form) into law. The first presented far less difficulty, especially when, following an unsuccessful attempt in 1896 (by a Conservative Government) to create new local authorities, it was decided to postpone that issue and to bring in a Bill whose sole purpose was to create a single central authority. This, everyone agreed, was the absolutely essential preliminary to the establishment of local authorities. 'What I should propose', wrote the Duke of Devonshire, who as Lord President of the Privy Council was nominally responsible for all elementary education, in a memorandum to the Cabinet, 'would be simply to take power to create a central authority to which might be transferred by Order in Council all the duties and powers of the Education Department, the Science and Art Department and such of the powers of the Charity Commissioners as relate to education.'[29] That was simple—once the objections of the Charity Commissioners to losing powers they valued had been overcome: and this was done, characteristically, by postponing the issue. The Board of Education Act reached the Statute Book in August 1899, and the Board began its work in April 1900.

Months before that the then Vice-President of the Committee of Council, Sir John Gorst, and the young civil servant whom he had made his private secretary, Robert Morant, had begun their tortuous underground manoeuvres[30] to bring about the abolition of the School Boards. Every history of English education tells how they succeeded, with the aid of the so-called 'Cockerton judgment' they had engineered, and of A. J. Balfour's decision that he would himself (assisted by Morant, back-stage) pilot through Parliament the highly controversial Education Bill of 1902. These well-known stories need not be retold here. Suffice to say that the 1902 Act gave public education in England and Wales an entirely new administrative and financial structure, and that the Prime Minister appointed its architect, Robert Morant, to be Permanent Secretary of the new Board of Education, with the task of building the structure into a system. How that arrogant man of genius carried out his assignment is the subject of the next chapter.

Notes

1. *Education in Great Britain*, 5th edn., Oxford University Press, 1967, p. 103.
2. Quoted from Asher Tropp. *The School Teachers: The Growth of the Teaching Profession in England and Wales from 1800 to the present day*, Heinemann, 1957, p. 111n.
3. Schools Inquiry Commission Report, vol. I, pp. 548–9.
4. Section 12.
5. Originally a joint stock company, it was in 1906 converted into a Trust: the Girls' Public Day School Trust (GPDST).
6. Vivian Hughes. *A London Girl of the Eighties*, Oxford University Press, 1936, p. 44. Quoted from Anne Ridler. *Olive Willis and Downe House*, Murray, 1967, pp. 75–6.
7. *Differentiation of Curricula between the Sexes in Secondary Schools*, HMSO, 1923.
8. *Education of Girls*, Faber, 1948. See also Kathleen Ollerenshaw. *Education for Girls*, Faber 1961, and Josephine Kamm. *Hope Deferred: girls' education in English history*, Methuen, 1965.
9. Josephine Kamm. *How Different from Us*, Bodley Head, 1958, p. 20.
10. Blanche Athena Clough. *A Memoir of Anne Jemima Clough*, Edward Arnold, 1903, p. 117.
11. Thomas Kelly, *A History of Adult Education in Great Britain*, Liverpool University Press, 1962, pp. 220–1.
12. Quoted from J. W. Adamson. *English Education 1789–1902*, Cambridge University Press, 1930, p. 291. The memorial is printed in full in the Commission's Report, vol. ii, pp. 194 ff.
13. Quoted from R. L. Archer. *Secondary Education in the Nineteenth Century*, Cambridge University Press, 1937, p. 236.
14. Professor of Moral Philosophy in the University, and a leading advocate of higher education for women.
15. Alice Zimmern. *The Renaissance of Girls' Education*, A. D. Innes, 1898, p. 117; quoted from Adamson, *op. cit.*, p. 333.
16. Chapters in the *History of Owens College and Manchester University 1851–1914*, Manchester University Press, 1937, p. 8.
17. Excerpts from Owens's will are quoted from H. B. Charlton. *Portrait of a University 1851–1951*, 2nd edn., Manchester University Press, 1952, p. 26.
18. A. Temple Patterson. *The University of Southampton*, published by the University, 1962, p. 12. I am indebted to Mr Patterson for the whole of this account of the origins of Southampton University.
19. H. C. Dent. *Universities in Transition*, Cohen and West, 1961, p. 52. The abolition of the Chair of Music was not quite so simple as the above quotation suggests. The Professor, Joseph Parry, was 'erratic and impulsive', and there was trouble over the students he accepted.
20. *British Universities*, Oxford University Press, 1966, p. 26.
21. A. N. Shimmin. *The University of Leeds. The first half-century*, published for the University by the Cambridge University Press, 1954, p. 11.
22. From the Deed of Settlement of Firth College, dated 20 May 1879. Quoted from A. W. Chapman. *The Story of a Modern University*, Oxford University Press, 1955, p. 13.
23. Quoted from Archer. *Secondary Education in the Nineteenth Century*, p. 263.
24. *Ibid.*, p. 261.

5

25. In *South Kensington to Robbins*, Longmans, 1964, p. 39.
26. Archer. *Secondary Education in the Nineetenth Century*, p. 307.
27. Sir G. W. Kekewich. *The Education Department and After*, Constable, 1920.
28. *Ibid.*, p. 53.
29. Quoted from P. H. J. H. Gosden. *The Development of Educational Administration in England and Wales*, Blackwell, 1966, pp. 87–8.
30. Unravelled by Eric Eaglesham, in *From School Board to Local Authority*, Routledge & Kegan Paul, 1956.

3

Decade of Change

Sir Robert Morant, one of the outstanding figures of all times in the English Civil Service.

Abraham Flexner.[1]

... a man of demoniac energy, with a consuming passion for work ... possessed of an equal determination to make others work with him, for him, or under him ... he was the oddest, if also one of the greatest, of all civil servants.

Professor E. J. R. Eaglesham.[2]

The rise of Robert Morant to a position of ultimate responsibility was rapid, and ruthless. He owed it in part to the fact that he had a gift for making influential acquaintances and of convincing them that because of his sheer intellectual capacity, initiative, and drive he was eminently worth advancing. By this means he became in 1899 private secretary to Sir John Gorst, the brilliant but erratic and indiscreet Vice-President of the Committee of Council, and in 1901 made personal contact with A. J. Balfour, then First Lord of the Treasury. Balfour was so impressed that he invited Morant to submit drafts for parliamentary Bills designed to effect a thorough reform of secondary education. Morant had his plans ready; he had been maturing them since 1898, if not earlier. In that year, when he was still working as deputy director in the Education Department's Branch of Special Inquiries and Reports, he included in a report on Swiss education:

... a devastating attack on the then organization of English education. He showed how one department was competing with another, and how the relationship between the central bodies and school boards was ill-defined; how in fact English educational administration was an unplanned, illogical, muddled confusion without clear responsibilities, duties or powers.[3]

57

It was into this report that Morant inserted an allegation that the School Boards were using the ratepayers' money illegally by spending it on higher grade schools, which were giving what was in effect secondary education, whereas the 1870 Act empowered them to spend rates on elementary education only. There was nothing new in this allegation. The Education Department had long known that the legality of such expenditure was suspect; but had in general condoned if not actively encouraged it. But now the allegation was being made, in a publication sponsored by the Department, as a deliberate attack on the School Boards. Moreover, Morant took care to bring the passage to the attention of known enemies of the School Boards—in particular Sir John Gorst and Dr William Garnett, secretary of the London Technical Education Board. The result was the well-known 'Cockerton' judgment, whereby the courts of law pronounced, and confirmed on appeal, that the London School Board's expenditure of money raised by rates on education other than elementary was illegal. This made radical change of the law relating to education obligatory.

Morant had ready not only plans for such reform, but the strategy and the tactics to get them translated into an Act of Parliament. His strategy was to secure Balfour as pilot of the Bill through Parliament because, as he wrote to him in September 1901, 'unless *you* are going to take the helm in Education next Session, and before the Session, nothing will be done successfully'.[4] His tactics were himself to master perfectly all the intricate details of the controversial matters that would arise in Parliament and to feed Balfour so fully and skilfully with argument that nothing but success could ensue. He achieved both aims. Balfour, excited by the prospect of a rare intellectual adventure, sloughed off the indolence which so often obscured his great ability, and from 24 March 1902, when he introduced the Bill into the Commons, until 18 December, when it passed into law, he 'showed himself the untiring and invincible debater he could be when he pleased'.[5] His was a superb performance, as anyone who cares to browse through Hansard will discover with delight. But the principal credit for the Education Act of 1902 must go to Morant, and to the one or two other people, notably Sidney Webb and Dr William Garnett, who knew precisely what they wanted to do,[6] and could envisage at least some of the revolutionary consequences of the measure they so largely helped to compile. Balfour did not, as he later half admitted. But he did know how to reward expertise. The Act was due to come into operation on 1 April 1903. In the autumn of 1902— before the Bill had even been finally approved by the Commons— Balfour asked Sir George Kekewich, Permanent Secretary to the

Board of Education, to go on paid leave between 1 November 1902 and 1 April 1903, when he was due to retire. He made Morant Acting Secretary for those six months and confirmed his appointment as Permanent Secretary in April 1903.

During the eight and a half years he spent in that post Morant transformed the English educational system. It would, of course, be wrong to ascribe to him all the changes that were brought about in that period, or even to suggest that he played the leading part in all. But, with the solitary exception of Sir James Kay-Shuttleworth (who was in office for just about the same length of time), no English civil servant has so effectively dominated the Education Department, or so comprehensively dictated its policy.

The greatness of Morant's achievement can be fairly assessed only if one remembers the obstacles and handicaps with which he had to contend. First, the 1902 Act contained several trouble-making compromises. (What principal Education Act passed in England does not?) The dual system of administration it created by adding to the county and county borough councils as local education authorities a large number of municipal borough and urban district councils, but limiting their powers to elementary education only, caused a great deal of vexation throughout the forty-two years up to 1944, when these 'Part III Authorities' were abolished. The concordat agreed between the State and the Churches which enabled voluntary schools to be assisted out of local rates did not satisfy either the Anglican or the Roman Catholic Church, and was bitterly contested for years by nonconformists, especially the 'Passive Resisters' who, led by the formidable Baptist minister, Dr John Clifford, allowed their household goods to be distrained rather than support 'Rome on the rates'. (I well remember seeing this, and the defiant slogan 'No Surrender!' displayed on large boards in front of their houses by citizens whose furniture had been seized for non-payment of rates.) But the Liberal Government returned in 1905 with the largest parliamentary majority ever known (including the unappeasable David Lloyd George, spearhead of Welsh opposition to the Act) found itself unable to alter this part of the law, though it tried hard enough.

A third compromise which could have proved exceedingly troublesome was that which made permissive only the powers granted to the LEAs to supply, or aid the supply of, 'education other than elementary', that is, secondary and further education, including the training of teachers. No statutory obligation was placed on the LEAs to provide or assist the provision of any form of education except elementary education. The grant of permissive powers to local authorities has always been something of a risk, for it may mean that while progressive (or extravagant) authorities get on with the job, even too rapidly or too largely in some cases, laggard or miserly authorities can, with a clear conscience, do little or nothing, knowing full well that the central government, however much it may cajole or threaten, is powerless to coerce them. The danger of such disparity of provision was far greater during the early years of the present century than it is today; the LEAs were new, and many of them ignorant; public education was neither well understood nor popular; innumerable councillors got elected by promising to 'keep down the rates'; and the Board of Education had no authority to compel: its statutory function was simply to 'supervise'. So it was fortunate for English education that for the first eight years of the new era it was directed by a man of clear vision and dynamic energy, a man who goaded progressive and laggard LEAs alike into incessant action.

Creating a secondary system

There can be little doubt that Morant's supreme achievement was his creation of a statutory system of secondary education. About the wisdom of the so-called 'academic bias' he is alleged to have given this system (and the extent to which he was personally responsible for this) people still dispute. 'The most salient defect in the new Regulations for Secondary Schools issued in 1904', wrote Dr Robert Fitzgibbon Young[7] in the historical chapter of the Spens Report, 'is that they failed to take note of the comparatively rich experience of secondary curricula of a practical and quasi-vocational type which had been evolved in the Higher Grade Schools, the Organized Science Schools and the Technical Day Schools'.

On the other hand, as Professor W. H. G. Armytage has written:[8]

The shortcomings of the old higher grade schools, with their excessive emphasis on scientific subjects, was condemned by HMIs and professional associations of teachers as one-sided, and detrimental to more humanistic and literary studies. Moreover, there was a growing demand for clerks, pupil-teachers and commercial recruits. So, after a Commons debate in July 1903, new regulations were issued to ensure that such an imbalance should not recur.

However much opinions may differ about Morant's part (or wisdom) in slanting maintained secondary education towards the literary curriculum of the public and endowed grammar schools, there can be no question about the magnitude of his achievement in creating a statutory system. In 1902, just before the Education Act became operative, the Board of Education was recognizing for grant 272 secondary schools containing 31,716 pupils. Ten years later it was recognizing over 1000, containing nearly 190,000 pupils—six times as many. And the increase in the number of schools and scholars was the least remarkable feature of this achievement. It is next to impossible, sixty or more years later, to give any realistic idea of the heterogeneity of the aggregation of schools which Morant welded, within a few short years, into a recognizable system with considerable unity of purpose: shabby genteel yet incredibly snobbish endowed grammar schools,[9] driven by poverty alone into the life-giving embrace of the LEAs; private 'secondary' schools, many equally snobbish, of all grades of quality from excellent to indifferent, or worse;[10] pupil-teacher centres, some very good, some mere cram shops; higher grade and higher elementary schools, including 'organized science schools' in which fifteen hours or more a week might be allocated to scientific subjects; and entirely new 'municipal' secondary schools conjured out of the rates by the recently created LEAs. The last could be not the least difficult, for many LEAs, inexperienced, and even brash though they might be, had strong (and often strange) ideas about the kinds of secondary school they wanted, and how they meant to run them—ideas which by no means always coincided with those of Morant and his colleagues at the Board of Education. In respect of curriculum many thought in terms of trade schools, in respect of government that, having built (or bought) the schools they could treat them as pieces of municipal property.

> Some of them planned to run all their secondary schools through a single sub-committee of governors. They gave their headmasters much more restricted powers than those enjoyed by heads of public schools. The headmasters . . . were subordinated to the director of education and his office.[11]

That is putting it mildly; some heads were treated like junior clerks. Much of the grammar school's dread of local authority control dates from this period.

To understand fully why the numbers of maintained schools, and scholars, grew with such spectacular rapidity between 1904 and 1914 it is essential to realize that large numbers of additional teachers were needed to improve the staffing of the elementary schools. The LEAs had quickly discovered that the voluntary schools, for whose maintenance they were responsible, were, in general, much worse staffed than the Board schools, both as to the number and the quality of their teachers. Morant himself was keenly concerned to improve the qualifications and raise the status of the elementary school teacher. To produce well-educated teachers it was absolutely necessary to give aspirants to the profession a considerably longer, and much better, secondary education than most of them were getting at the time. An essential part of this improvement had to be the ending of their segregation in pupil-teacher centres; the secondary education of pupil-teachers must be in company with pupils expecting to follow other careers. This was no new thinking; to go no farther back than 1898, the Departmental Committee which reported in that year on the pupil-teacher system had said so quite explicitly.

It is extremely desirable that all intending teachers should pass through a secondary school for the completion of their ordinary education (p. 6).

We do not think that the pupil-teacher centres, under present conditions, adequately fulfil the purposes of secondary schools; they are, rather, substitutes and supplements in an imperfect system . . . (p. 7).

We look forward to the ultimate conversion of those centres which are well staffed and properly equipped into real secondary schools, where, although perhaps intending teachers may be in the majority, they will have ampler time for their studies, and will be instructed side by side with pupils who have other careers in view. (p. 8).

Morant set out to end the pupil-teacher system. This could not have been done in 1898, for there were not nearly enough efficient secondary schools to have absorbed anything approaching the 30,000 pupil-teachers. It could not be done all at once in 1903, when Morant began to make known his intentions. There were still not sufficient secondary schools. The operation had to be conducted in stages; and the more one studies Morant's moves the more one admires his skill— and is consequently less amazed at the speed with which he was able to carry through these stages.

The first shots in his campaign were fired in 1903. The Board's *Regulations for the Instruction and Training of Pupil-Teachers and Students in Training Colleges*,[12] issued in July, gave notice that:

(i) from 1 August 1904 no pupils under 16 years old would be accepted as pupil-teachers, except in rural areas, where they could be accepted, if HMI agreed, at 15.

(ii) from 1 August 1905 no pupil-teachers would be allowed to serve in an elementary school for 'more than half the time the school is open' (i.e., not more than half the school week was to be devoted to teaching).

(iii) unless 'long distances or defective travelling arrangements' made it impossible, pupil-teachers must spend the other half of the school week in a recognized Pupil-Teacher centre.

The purpose of these Regulations, wrote Morant in the 'Prefatory Memorandum' he contributed to them, is 'to secure for the Pupil-Teacher a more complete and continuous education, and to make the period of service in an Elementary School a time of probation and training rather than of too early practice in teaching'. The Regulations, he said, were based on two principles: (i) deferral of employment as a teacher in an elementary school to allow more time for the pupil-teacher's general education, and (ii) the continuance of that education, under reasonable circumstances (i.e. in a pupil-teacher centre), during the period of apprenticeship.

Free places

Morant did not forget the financial aspect; he realized it was necessary to ensure that the parents of prospective pupil-teachers could afford to postpone putting their children into paid employment—a serious consideration in days of low wages, and virtually no statutory social services. He therefore urged LEAs to arrange:

> by means of an adequate scholarship system or otherwise, that all the cleverest candidates for Pupil-Teacherships . . . whether boys or girls, should receive a sound general education in a Secondary School for three or four years, with schoolfellows intended for other careers, before they commence service in any capacity in an Elementary School.[13]

To the credit of the LEAs, be it said, many responded promptly and generously to this appeal. (Some, London in particular, had been offering such scholarships since their School Board days.) So much so that when in 1907, in response to persistent criticism in Parliament that far too few scholarships to secondary schools were being awarded, the Liberal Government introduced the 'free place' scheme,[14] this did not at first greatly increase the proportion of scholarship holders. Under this scheme the Board of Education offered larger grants to secondary schools which reserved annually a substantial proportion of places (ordinarily the equivalent of one quarter of the previous year's intake) for pupils from public elementary schools whose tuition fees would be paid by their LEAs. These pupils, it was understood, would not be *scholarship* winners. They would not have to *compete* for their places; they would only have to pass a *qualifying* examination. Such was the intention. Alas! within a very few years the 'free place' examination had already become in many areas intensely competitive.

Actually, in 1906 some 24 per cent of the pupils in grant-aided secondary schools were ex-elementary school pupils whose fees were being paid for them, mainly by LEAs. The introduction of the 'free place' scheme was, however, extremely valuable because of the principle upon which it was based. That principle was that 'all secondary schools aided by grants shall be made fully accessible to children of all classes'—not, as previously, only to (i) those whose parents could afford to pay the (admittedly modest) tuition fees, or (ii) were grant-aided by public authorities for some specific reason—e.g. that they intended to become teachers in maintained schools, or (iii) were assisted by private charity. The proportion of 'free place' pupils proposed by the Board of Education and accepted by Parliament was a bitter disappointment to the Trades Union Congress, and other working-class organizations, which had for ten years or more been campaigning for 'secondary education for all'. It is easy today to see how right the TUC was, but in 1907 the country as a whole was certainly not prepared to accept this policy. Nor, indeed, was the working-class movement as a whole; there was widespread suspicion (not altogether unjustified) of secondary schools, as middle-class institutions, not for working people. In fact, the liberalization of the governmental attitude implied by the radical change from admission to secondary school for working-class children only if they were of 'exceptional quality' to admission for all 'qualified to profit' was probably as much as most sections of public opinion would stomach. Some, including, unhappily, many secondary school teachers, found it extremely unpalatable. Some grammar schools relinquished their grants rather than accept 'free-placers'. Others treated free-placers like pariahs, even teaching them in separate classes—until they began to discover that these ex-elementary school pupils were on the whole abler, that they stayed longer at school, worked harder, and secured more university scholarships than the generality of fee-paying pupils.

To ensure that as many pupil-teachers as possible should get 'a more complete and continuous' general education, in company with 'schoolfellows intended for other careers', Morant adopted from the start the policy of doing away with segregated pupil-teacher centres.

He did this in three ways: (i) by persuading secondary schools to establish pupil-teacher centres, (ii) by amalgamating pupil-teacher centres with secondary schools, or (iii) if neither of these means was practicable, by closing down centres and transferring the pupil-teachers to secondary schools. Despite bitter opposition from considerable numbers of teachers and LEA administrators, he achieved a swift and signal success. In the year 1905–6, of a total of 482 recognized pupil-teacher centres 283 were integral parts of secondary schools and 192 were separately organized. Four years later, in 1909–10, of 603 recognized centres 512 were integrated in secondary schools, and only 80 were separately organized.

This part of the build-up of the statutory system of secondary education is susceptible of exact measurement. The development of the secondary school curriculum is not. In this matter Morant was for many years consistently featured as the villain in the piece, the hidebound traditionalist who imposed upon the new secondary system the academic and literary curriculum he had been brought up on at Winchester, the curriculum of the public and the endowed grammar school. It is now realized, however, as the quotation from Professor Armytage on page 60 shows, that a very considerable body of educational opinion, including HMIs, leaned towards that type of curriculum as a corrective to the excessive specialization in science which took place in some Higher Grade schools. Mrs Olive Banks, in her illuminating study of *Parity and Prestige in English Secondary Education*,[15] suggests another, most intriguing, reason for the adoption of an academic and literary rather than a scientific and practical curriculum. (It must be noted, incidentally, that the curriculum laid down in the 1904 Regulations was not so 'literary and academic' as is often implied. It required a minimum of 7½ hours a week of science and mathematics—the same as for the group of subjects consisting of English, geography, history and one foreign language.)

> It is likely that the strongest pressure away from a scientific and towards an academic curriculum during these years at the beginning of the century came from the central role assigned to the secondary schools in the education of the future pupil teachers . . . (p. 44).

'The Board of Education', said the *Journal of Education* in December 1903, 'should have the wit to perceive, even if the individual County Council does not, that it cannot be a good thing to train up all would-be pupil-teachers upon a curriculum in which science and mathematics are exalted at the expense of the humanities.'

In fact the local authorities did perceive this very well, and there is every possibility that it lay behind their preference for the literary type of curriculum (p. 49). . . .

This is another illustration of the fact, too often ignored, that the causes of change in education, as in every other field of the national life, are far more complex than many of us admit, or even know. It is so easy (and emotionally satisfying) to portray Morant as the machiavellian aristocrat who single-handedly imposed the Establishment curriculum upon the non-U municipal secondary school. But it appears that not only had HM Inspectorate and university and secondary school teachers (who might also be Establishment) a hand in this, but also Parliament and the local education authorities . . .

New ideas

When one passes from legislative and organizational change to change in the content of the curriculum, the teaching methods, and the personal relationships between teachers and taught one finds it far more difficult to be precise about what happened during this crucial first decade of the twentieth century. For two main reasons. First, the changes in the law and in the administration of public education in England and Wales are fully documented in easily accessible primary sources—annual reports, codes of regulations, circulars and memoranda—and have been digested in great detail by professional historians. For scrutiny of change in curricula and methods few such precise sources of information exist. Works by reformers and their adherents are often opinionated, and sometimes incoherent, those of their critics little better. And historians have, unfortunately, given far less attention to these aspects of change. Secondly, the winds of curricular and methodological change usually begin to blow as barely perceptible breezes. They were already rustling intermittently through English education in the 1890s. They gathered increasing strength during that decade and the next. It is no exaggeration to say that never before in the history of English education (and possibly never since) have so many and such various influences making for change played so vigorously upon the teacher as during the first decade of the twentieth century.

Among these influences must be mentioned the ideas and experiments of John Dewey, W. H. Kilpatrick, Stanley Hall, E. L. Thorndike and other American philosophers and psychologists whose work became generally known in Britain round the turn of the century.

(Nor, of course, should the earlier, widely pervasive, influence of William James be overlooked.) From France a few years later came news of a very different but equally revolutionary development: a French professor, Alfred Binet, had devised a standard scale for measuring human intelligence. Mental testing was quickly taken up in England by a number of able young men, including Cyril Burt, whom the London County Council in 1913 appointed as their educational psychologist—the first such appointment in the United Kingdom.

During the closing years of the nineteenth century and the early years of the twentieth the English Froebelians radically modernized their kindergarten programme. Hardly had they completed this modernization before news began to reach our shores of an original method of educating young children which was being developed by an Italian medical practitioner, Dr Maria Montessori. But long before the Froebelian renaissance or the Montessori revelation, way back in the 1890s two American-born Scottish sisters, Margaret and Rachel McMillan, had begun in Bradford a crusade on behalf of children's health which possibly did more to change for the better the face of English education than any other movement of the time. The McMillans were eagerly assisted by Dr James Kerr, whom Bradford had appointed (quite illegally) in 1892 as the Council's school medical officer. Together, the three campaigned for school meals, school medical inspection, school baths, open-air schools and camp schools. Early in the twentieth century the sisters moved to London, where among other like-minded friends of children they met Mrs Humphrey Ward, daughter of Thomas Arnold, who had started 'vacation schools' for children who otherwise had only the streets in which to play, F. W. Jowett, a Labour MP who was later to introduce into Parliament a Private Member's Bill which became the Provision of Meals Act, 1906, Albert Mansbridge, founder of the WEA, and—Robert Morant.

The McMillans' work in London tended increasingly to be on behalf of the youngest children. As Rachel said, after the success of their 'camp schools' for older girls and boys (on a litter-covered piece of waste ground at Deptford): 'We must begin further back, with the children and their mothers before the little ones come to school. Five years old is too late.'[16]

One of the soldiers returned from the Boer war, Colonel R. S. Baden-Powell, may not have altogether agreed. In 1907 he gathered a group of boys in a camp on Brownsea Island in Poole Harbour, taught them a peaceful version of the scouting techniques he had learned on active service in South Africa—and launched a movement which spread swiftly, not only throughout the British Isles but all over the world. Baden-Powell provided only for boys; within three years girls had formed their own association, and induced his wife to head it.

The Boy Scouts' and Girl Guides' Associations catered for children's leisure time, but it was not long before their activities found their way into school hours. In 1925 the afternoon a week devoted to Scout and Cadet work was already an established institution in the secondary school where I was teaching. But many years earlier attempts had begun, chiefly though not exclusively in private schools, to transform lessons into, if not leisure at any rate pleasure, chiefly by making children active partners with their teachers in the pursuit of knowledge and skill. English pioneers in this field were Cecil Reddie, who founded a school at Abbotsholme in Derbyshire in 1889, and J. H. Badley, who after an apprenticeship at Abbotsholme (in which he found some of his ideas fundamentally at variance with those of Reddie) moved south with his wife in 1893 to start in Sussex—at first as a boys' school only, but from 1898 as a coeducational boarding school—the still well-known Bedales School, since 1900 located near Petersfield in Hampshire.

Reddie, Badley, and other radically-minded reformers, such as the ex-HMIs Beatrice Ensor and Edmond Holmes, and the arch-revolutionary A. S. Neill, during the first three decades of the twentieth century did English education a profoundly valuable service by insisting that freedom belongs to children as well as to adults. But even in the 1890s private schools were not the only 'free' schools, though their less humble protagonists have always appeared to assume so. In public elementary schools here and there initiative and spontaneity began to emerge, thanks to successive relaxations of the Revised Code, and the encouragement given by Kekewich and members of HM Inspectorate. About the part Morant later played in nurturing this new spirit there are conflicting opinions. Professor Eaglesham, an authority on the period between 1870 and the 1914–18 war, says: 'A cynic might argue that . . . *Morant aimed at and achieved a standstill in elementary education.* There is evidence to support such a conclusion.'[17] Yet he concedes that the Board of Education—i.e. Morant—gave elementary education 'a plan', 'and thereby set its house in order', and he regards this as an 'important contribution'.[18] I venture to think that Morant did more than this, that he gave to the public elementary school an inspiring ideal at which to aim, and to its teachers a professional freedom without precedent in England or any other country. 'The purpose of the Public Elementary School', he wrote in the Preface to its 1904 Code of Regulations, 'is to form and strengthen the character and to develop the intelligence of the children entrusted to it, and to make the best use of the school years available, in assisting both boys and girls, according to their different needs to fit themselves, practically as well as intellectually, for the work of life'.

Professor Eaglesham calls this aim 'a general one'.[19] So it is, and for that reason how much better than the narrowly particular aims which were all that many (perhaps most) elementary school teachers pursued at that time. I was a pre-adolescent pupil in an elementary school in 1904. Like millions more, I intoned my way monotonously (and uncomprehendingly) through the multiplication tables; I was bored to nausea by the one and only 'Reader' we were allowed each year—which had to serve the dual function of giving us practice in the mechanics of reading aloud (why aloud?) and of being our introduction to English life and letters. I wrote, endlessly, in 'copy-books' morally elevating maxims—'A stitch in time saves nine', 'Too many cooks spoil the broth'—but I never composed, much less wrote, in class a single original sentence. I memorized, in rhyme, the names and idiosyncrasies of the English kings and queens

> William the Conqueror long did reign,
> William his son by an arrow was slain . . .

and I memorized (though not in rhyme) the names of the capes, bays, county towns, mountains and rivers, literally all round Britain. And once each week I painted blobs (we called them flowers), and wove wet reeds into work baskets: the school's sole concessions to 'activity'.

Not much in all that to 'form and strengthen the character', or 'develop the intelligence', or 'make the best use of the school years', or fit children, either 'practically' or 'intellectually', 'for the work of life'. And this experience of mine, I must emphasize, was not in the class of a cynical, dull or apathetic teacher, but of a lively, intelligent, warm-hearted woman, who as a person did us boys and girls a world of good. Did she know no other way to teach? Or was she bound by the school timetable?—that sacroscant nineteenth-century visual aid, put up 'in a prominent position' (as the Code required) by the new head teacher when he arrived, and never taken down until he left, it might well be thirty years later. (Men did not move then as they do now. Nor did women, for that matter; the age of the 'dedicated spin-ster' was just beginning, as one LEA after another refused to employ married women.)

Such teaching as I endured went on for many years in many schools after 1904. The spirit outlived the fact of 'payment by results' in the practice of teachers who could not change their ways, even when they wanted to, which many did. But there were others, and their numbers grew with the years, who responded eagerly to the challenge thrown down, in 1905, in the first edition of the Board of Education's *Handbook of suggestions for the consideration of Teachers and others engaged in the Work of Public Elementary Schools*:

> The only uniformity of practice that the Board of Education desire to see in the teaching of Public Elementary Schools is that each teacher shall think for himself, and work out for himself such methods of teaching as may use his powers to the best advantage, and be best suited to the particular needs and conditions of the school.

Some teachers even dared to think that they and their pupils should be friends, not foes, should work with, not against, each other; and they initiated the most profoundly important transformation of the English elementary school, from a place of hatred to one of happiness.

Health services

If Morant's attitude towards the public elementary school as an educational institution be regarded as in some respects ambivalent, no one can suggest that there was any suspicion of ambivalence about his attitude to the physical health and wellbeing of the children who attended it. He may not have been primarily responsible for the introduction of the School Meals and School Medical Services. Albert Mansbridge always maintained that it was Margaret McMillan who got the Education (Provision of Meals) Act on to the Statute Book in 1906; but even that is a large oversimplification. School meals, medical inspection, the much less publicized development of health education (called 'hygiene'), improved physical training, improved teaching of cookery and other domestic subjects in elementary schools resulted in this decade from a combination of frightened public opinion and the activities of philanthropic, political, and educational pressure groups. Public opinion had been first perturbed by the large number of would-be recruits to the British Army during the Boer War who had been rejected because of poor health or physical disability, and later scared by a horrifying *Report on Physical Deterioration* published by the Government in 1904. The McMillan sisters and Dr James Kerr and their associates formed but one (though probably the most persistent) among many groups that had long been demanding (and providing) meals and medical care for undernourished and afflicted elementary school children. (It is indicative of the social gulf which existed between elementary education and secondary that no one suggested these welfare services for secondary schools.)

While Morant was far from being a prime mover in the campaign for school welfare services he was able to do much to unlock the parliamentary door. The cause lay near his heart. He had always been keenly interested in medical research, and especially in preventive medicine. He had got to know, and to respect, Margaret McMillan. When, therefore, she and her sister organized a deputation to the Liberal Government in 1906 to urge it to make statutory provision for school meals and medical inspection they already had powerful official support behind the scenes.

The Education (Provision of Meals) Act passed in 1906 was, unfortunately, only a permissive measure; it imposed no statutory obligation on LEAs to provide meals. It empowered them to assist voluntary bodies to provide, or themselves to provide, meals for children 'unable by reason of lack of food to take full advantage of the education provided for them'. (Section 3.) A modest charge was to be made for the meals to parents who could afford to pay. To enable LEAs to give necessitous children free meals the Act empowered them to levy a rate not exceeding one halfpenny in the pound for the purpose.

As the Act laid no statutory duty upon LEAs, and as no special machinery was set up, either at the centre or in the localities, school meals never really got off the ground until 1941, when the British Government made them part of the national policy for safeguarding children's health during the Second World War. Previously, except at one or two moments of massive unemployment, no more than 3 per cent of the children in public elementary schools (the Act did not extend to secondary schools) were at any given time receiving school meals. As most of these children were undernourished children the meals were widely regarded as a Poor Law charity, a belief which was frequently given colour both by the kind of meal provided (similar to that of the philanthropic soup kitchen) and by the fact that the children were marched away from the school to some other building to eat it.

The same stagnation might well have overcome the School Medical Service, which, indeed, almost failed to get born. A Government Bill which included provision for medical inspection on a permissive basis was passed by the Commons in 1906—but rejected by the House of Lords on the sacred grounds of economy and prudence. Happily, persistent pressure, from the McMillan group and Labour MPs in particular, secured for it a place in a private member's Bill in 1907, and it ultimately reached the Statute Book as an item in an Education (Miscellaneous Provisions) Act passed in 1907. Section 13(b) of this laid a duty upon LEAs: 'to provide for the medical inspection of children immediately before or at the time of or as soon as possible after their admission to a public elementary school, and on such other occasions as the Board of Education direct' and gave them power 'to make such arrangements as may be sanctioned by the Board of Education for attending to the health and physical condition of the children educated in Public Elementary Schools'. (Again, it will be noticed, no mention is made of secondary schools, although the same Act introduced the 'free place' scheme of transfer from elementary to secondary schools. It was not until 1918 that medical inspection, and in certain conditions treatment, for secondary school pupils were included.)

Morant took immediate and effective action. He established a medical department in the Board of Education, and persuaded Dr (later Sir) George Newman to head it. Never was a happier choice. Newman, who had learned the hard facts of life as medical officer in the poverty-stricken and overcrowded borough of Finsbury, combined a rare enthusiasm for his task with great gifts of organization and a genius for personal relations. His earlier annual Reports, with their appalling record of ill-health and physical defect among school children, bit deeply into the national conscience (or such part of it as was alive to the existence of social evils), and there can be little doubt that had not the First World War intervened the powers of the School Medical Service would have been substantially strengthened before 1918.

Dr Newman's massive contribution to children's good health comprised, of course, far more than making the public aware of its lack. He was a persistent advocate of positive measures: school clinics, open-air schools for delicate children, nursery schools for young children, better physical education in schools, better school buildings. When he retired in 1935 he might justly have claimed to have improved the health of the nation's children literally out of all recognition.

(I write this with a deep sense of personal gratitude. I lived as a child at school amidst the adenoids, the decayed teeth, the 'earache', the rickets, the 'rheumatism', the ringworm, the erysipelas and the ubiquitous fleas and lice that were such common afflictions among elementary school children in the first decade of the twentieth century.)

Technical education neglected

'For some years after 1902 the efforts of the State and of the local education authorities were mainly devoted to augmenting the supply of secondary schools'.[20] It was perhaps inevitable that, with so many and such massive reforms going ahead, some part of the educational system should be neglected. In the first two decades of the twentieth century the chosen victim was technical education. It was cold-shouldered by the Board of Education, which until 1918 made it no grants for capital expenditure. It was cold-shouldered by the LEAs, who, having to find formidable sums for building secondary schools, were in no position to bear the total cost of buildings and equipment for technical colleges. It was cold-shouldered by the upper and middle classes of a society whose 'whole ethos', it has been said, 'was directed towards "respectable" white-collar jobs'.[21] (Yet this was the era in which England had to import thousands of German clerks to get its business correspondence done and its ledgers written up.)

But though no large advances were made in any part of the vast field of vocational education, there were several interesting developments, little regarded at the time, that were later to expand into important movements. The first of these in point of time was the gradual adoption from 1902 onwards, and in the north of England to begin with, of 'grouped' courses, that is, courses composed of related subjects, in place of haphazard individual choices based on what a student thought he fancied or—only too often—the fact that some subjects were available at the local 'tech' but others were not. These grouped courses had three great advantages: first, they gave students a sense of purpose, direction and security, since they clearly led towards proficiency in specific occupations or groups of occupations; secondly, they enabled technical schools and colleges to plan rational programmes of studies instead of trying to provide a sufficiently heterogeneous cafeteria service to meet every customer's whim; thirdly, they induced men of better ability to become technical college principals; and they in turn attracted better staff and demanded better equipment—all of which enhanced the reputation of their colleges. Grouped courses were made Board of Education policy in 1910, had been adopted by most LEAs before the First World War, and after it formed the foundation on which was built the scheme of National Certificates and Diplomas.

A second development was the rise in the early years of the century of daytime classes in technical colleges for boys (and some girls) wishing to learn particular trades. These classes, which accepted pupils at thirteen-plus, or sometimes even earlier, were officially recognized, though with no enthusiasm, by the Board of Education in 1905 as 'day technical classes'. In this twilight existence they lived until 1913. During these eight years they separated themselves into two distinct groups. In London they remained definitely 'trade schools', preparing children vocationally for a particular occupation. Elsewhere—in Manchester, for example—they tended to become schools which, while they had a strong bias towards a group of occupations (engineering, building, and secretarial work were the commonest), nevertheless included in their curriculum a considerable amount of general education.

In 1913 the Board of Education (no longer under Morant's direction) decided that it ought to give the day technical classes a status (and a grant) 'more commensurate to their importance'. The result was an almost ludicrous illustration of the social and educational stratification in Edwardian society. The 'junior technical schools', as they were renamed, were put firmly in their (inferior) place. They were most definitely not secondary schools. It was emphatically not their business to prepare pupils for entry into university or any other form of higher education. Their ambit was confined to the lower rungs of the vocational ladder, their function to preparing boys for artisan and comparable industrial occupations, girls for domestic service.

Somehow the junior technical schools survived; but despite their generally excellent record in placing pupils in skilled and responsible employment, not until 1938 (in the Spens Report) were their virtues properly recognized or rewarded.

Triple alliance

If vocational education had a thin time during the first decade of the twentieth century, non-vocational 'adult' education had what will probably always rank as its finest hour. In 1898 Albert Mansbridge, a young man of twenty-two, employed as a clerk by the Co-operative Wholesale Society, delivered at a congress arranged by the Co-operative Movement a rather remarkable address which attracted the attention of Michael Sadler, and brought him an invitation to speak at the forthcoming University Extension summer meeting. He accepted the invitation, and at Oxford expounded his great idea: a grand alliance between the University, through its Extra-Mural Delegacy, and the Co-operative Movement to provide a national service of non-vocational adult education for working-class men and women. The idea was not too well received—possibly because of Mansbridge's vehemence in advocating it. Or so he thought in later years. 'I advocated this so whole-heartedly', he wrote, 'as almost to wreck for the time being the cause I had at heart.'[22]

Mansbridge was wise enough to profit by his failure. But he did not abandon his idea; he expanded it. In three articles published in the *University Extension Journal* during the spring of 1903 he proposed a triple alliance: University Extension, the Trade Unions, and the Co-operative Movement. In the third article he wrote: 'In order fully to test the proposals herein made, it will probably be well for a pioneer association to be initiated, which will so work as to endeavour to render a permanent association inevitable.'[23] On the 16th day of the same month, May 1903, Albert Mansbridge and his wife Frances founded, over a cup of tea at the British Museum, the 'pioneer association': The Association to promote the Higher Education of Working Men, primarily by the Extension of University Teaching; also by (i) Development of an efficient School Continuation system; (ii) the assistance of Working-class Efforts of a specifically educational character.

This time Mansbridge's idea was almost rapturously welcomed. In August a conference at Oxford unanimously resolved that: 'The necessary Higher Education of the Working Classes will best be furthered by an associated effort on the part of the Trade Unions, Co-operative Societies, and Extension Authorities.'[24] Within twelve months Mansbridge's membership of two (himself and his wife) had rocketed to 146, made up of 135 individual members and 11 Co-operative societies. In October 1904 the first local branches were formed, at Reading and Rochdale—the latter once again in the vanguard of advance. Here, an Education Guild organized during its first twelve months an almost unbelievably large and varied programme of activities.

In August 1905 the Association dropped its cumbrous original title, and chose the strikingly simple one of the Workers' Educational Association (WEA). Mansbridge was made the fulltime general secretary (at a salary of less than one pound a week), and 'his little office in his home at Ilford became the centre of a far-reaching network of organization and propaganda'.[25] Within two years the WEA had 4343 individual members and 622 affiliated societies. By 1914 these had increased to 11,430 individual members and 2555 affiliated societies, grouped in 179 local branches.

But the significant growth was not in numbers, spectacular though this was. No greater error could be made than to measure the success of the WEA, even in its earliest days, by counting heads. Its success lay in the quality of the teaching it provided and of the learning it evoked. Its most significant breakthrough came in 1908; and the credit for this must go jointly to the Rochdale Education Guild, which put up the scheme, Albert Mansbridge, who saw its possibilities, R. H. Tawney, then a young lecturer at Glasgow University, and the members of his classes at Rochdale in Lancashire and Longton in Staffordshire, who magnificently made it a reality.

The story of the starting of the 'three-year tutorial' classes is, briefly, as follows. In 1906 the Rochdale Education Guild, not finding the normal series of university extension lectures meeting their needs satisfactorily, submitted to Mansbridge, as secretary of the WEA, a scheme for a course, of some length, of 'tutorial classes' which would involve a working partnership between tutor and class. (A similar scheme had been advocated in London, and tried out experimentally at Battersea.) Mansbridge replied that if they could recruit a minimum of thirty people who were prepared to undertake a course of serious study at a high level extending over two years he would get them the best tutor available. Both sides fulfilled their promises; and in January 1908 Tawney began the first 'three-year tutorial'. (The duration of the course was early extended from two to three years.) By a quirk of history the very first class was not held at Rochdale, but at Longton—but only one day before the Rochdale meeting.

The WEA has always remained a minority movement, with its emphasis on quality of work, not number of students. In its early days the intellectual level was often very high, for the classes attracted many men and women who today would go as a matter of course to a university, but who never thought seriously of doing so because to all intents and purposes the opportunity did not exist. Yet during the very years in which Mansbridge was advocating his 'Association to promote the Higher Education of Working Men' the opportunity to secure a university education, modern in kind and modest in cost, was being dramatically enlarged by the first large-scale creation of universities the country had ever known.

Civic universities

Within nine years the number of universities in England was doubled, from five to ten. Such a large and rapid increase must obviously have resulted from deep-rooted causes, and the labours of many people. But one person above all others was responsible for starting it off: Joseph Chamberlain, MP, 'the uncrowned king of Birmingham',[26] reckoned by many people (not without reason since his splitting of the Liberal Party over Irish Home Rule) the most formidable politician in the country. In 1898 Mason College was made by Act of Parliament a university college, and Chamberlain became its first President. He set out at once to get it a university charter. He succeeded within two years, having in the meantime raised over £300,000 by public subscription. Elected the University's first Chancellor, he promptly appealed for another quarter of a million—and got it.

Birmingham's elevation was a decisive stimulus to Liverpool, which had never been happy in the Victoria federation. With the agreement of Owens College the federal university was dissolved. Liverpool University received its charter in 1903, and in the same year the Victoria University was reconstituted as a unitary body, built round Owens College. Leeds University College had objected strongly to the dissolution of the Manchester federation; the Privy Council overruled its objection, but offered Leeds the opportunity to submit a draft charter for 'a university in Yorkshire'. Leeds took this to mean that it was to be *the* University of Yorkshire; Sheffield University College, which had been repeatedly and rudely refused admission into the Victoria University, not surprisingly objected violently to this. In the end, matters were amicably settled; in 1904 and 1905 respectively Leeds and Sheffield were granted university charters.

Bristol took rather longer to secure its charter, partly because for a while, like Leeds, it harboured thoughts of becoming the head of a large territorial empire: of a West of England University, with headquarters in Bristol, and annexes at Exeter, Reading, and Southampton. But the proposed annexes firmly refused to play; small and weak they might still be, but they had their own aspirations, and they much preferred to pursue these, even though this might mean—as it did—a long wait.

Reading and Southampton had only recently, in 1902, received university college charters. Exeter had not got even that far; not until after the First World War, in 1922, did it become the University College of the South West, though its origins went back farther than those of most of the newly chartered universities. What gave both Exeter and Reading the ambition to aim at university status, was the strength of their university extension activities. These had led to the setting up in Reading in 1892 of a University Extension College in conjunction with the municipal Schools of Art and Science. The following year Exeter carried out a broadly similar amalgamation, uniting science, arts, and extension classes in a Technical and University Extension College. In 1899 this was renamed the Royal Albert

Memorial College, as had been the original building which the city erected in 1865 to house its art school, library, and museum.

Though Reading and Southampton were recognized for grant as university institutions in 1902, neither was considered strong enough either academically or financially to merit promotion to full university status. Nor was Nottingham—but for quite other reasons. The Town Council had made history in the 1870s, and the college which they had founded, and which they maintained, had borne the title 'University College' ever since they opened it in 1881. Unfortunately the civic pride which had prompted their pioneer venture operated to make them retain too strict control over it for too long. It was only after some complicated and delicate unloosening of their grip that the Privy Council could advise the King in 1903 to grant Nottingham a university college charter.

Complicated as were the Nottingham negotiations, they were child's play by comparison with the long drawn out and labyrinthine coils that had had to be unwoven before 'the great examination machine misnamed the University of London', as Professor Armytage has called it,[27] could become what it ought always to have been, a university in every sense of the term. No more than one or two of the innumerable twists and turns will be mentioned here. In 1884, prompted by the apparent success of the federal Victoria University, a group of university teachers, lawyers, and medical men formed an Association for Promoting a Teaching University for London, to be called the Albert University. In 1887 King's College and University College, both strongly opposed to the idea of a second university in London, petitioned the Privy Council for power to award their own degrees. The Government's reply was to appoint a Royal Commission. This recommended, in 1889, that the existing University of London should apply for a charter giving it teaching as well as examining powers. But—of all things!—the University itself could not agree about this. So in 1892 the Government appointed a second Royal Commission. In 1894 this made very much the same recommendations as the first: that there be one university only in London, that this be a teaching university, and that it be established by Act of Parliament. And there, but for one man, R. B. (later Viscount) Haldane, the matter might well have rested. Through four years Haldane persisted against all opposition—including that of the MP for London University. He drafted the necessary Bill for Parliament. He introduced it, and was defeated. Realizing that a private member's Bill stood no chance, he persuaded Balfour to sponsor a Government Bill. Even this might have failed had not Haldane made a remarkable impromptu speech at its second reading. He converted the Commons. The Bill was passed; and in January 1900 London became, at long last, a university with power to teach.

Not that its troubles were over. (The cynic might be tempted to suggest that they had only just begun.) But, though housed less than satisfactorily in South Kensington, it gradually gathered strength as one institution after another became affiliated with it. Not least important of its accessions was the Imperial College of Science and Technology, formed in 1907 by the administrative union of the Royal College of Science, the Royal School of Mines, and the City and Guilds Engineering College. Many people thought this federation might become an independent university; but it preferred to attach itself to London, to which it has remained faithful, despite more than one temptation to solitary grandeur.

In the forty-four years between 1870 and 1914 England built up, from what can best be described as ragged chaos, statutory systems of elementary and secondary education which, though in many respects inadequate and shot through with faults, at any rate functioned effectively. It had a system of further education in the making, and was developing a system of higher education. The foregoing pages have, it is hoped, given some slight idea, not only of the obstacles that had to be overcome, but also of the delays that these caused, delays which must have seemed unendurably long to those whose aims they frustrated. But seen historically the pace had been hot. With the set-back of the First World War it was to slacken markedly. The twenty years between 1918 and 1939 were to be a period of gestation rather than action. Not until 1944 was rapid advance resumed.

Notes

1. *Universities, American, English, German,* Oxford University Press, 1930, p. 226.
2. *The Foundations of 20th Century Education in England,* Routledge & Kegan Paul, 1967, p. 39.
3. Eaglesham, *op. cit.,* p. 40.
4. Quoted from John Leese. *Personalities and Power in English Education,* E. J. Arnold, 1950, p. 227. *Morant's italics.*
5. Elie Halévy. *History of the English People.* Epilogue: 1895–1905, Book 2, Penguin Books, 1939, p. 115.
6. See *The Education Muddle and The Way Out,* Fabian Tract 106, 1901.
7. Spens Report, p. 66. Dr R. F. Young, a historian of vast erudition, and an authority on Comenius, was the Secretary of the Consultative Committee of the Board of Education for all the three Hadow Reports as well as the Spens Report.

8. *Four Hundred Years of English Education*, p. 187.
9. Admirably portrayed in *For Sons of Gentlemen*, by 'Kerr Shaw' (pseudonym of Ronald Gurner, a secondary school headmaster), Dent, 1928.
10. I suffered as a pupil for a year in one that was much worse, and later 'taught' for a term in one that was incredibly bad. On the other hand I spent three happy years (1911–14) as an assistant master in one which, within its limitations, could hardly have been better.
11. Eaglesham. *Foundations* . . ., p. 57.
12. Command 1666, HMSO, 7 July 1903. This was the first time these Regulations were issued separately; they had previously formed part of the Elementary School Code.
13. Prefatory Memorandum, p. 9.
14. In the Education (Administrative Provisions) Act 1907.
15. Routledge & Kegan Paul, 1955. See Chapter 3, 'Sir Robert Morant and Secondary School Curricula', pp. 31–50.
16. Quoted from a booklet issued by the Rachel McMillan Training College in 1960 as a centenary tribute to Margaret McMillan, born in 1860.
17. Eaglesham. *Foundations* . . ., p. 51. *His italics*.
18. *Ibid.*, p. 52.
19. *Ibid.*, p. 53.
20. Report of the Board of Education for the year 1911–12.
21. Argles, Michael, *South Kensington to Robbins*. Longmans, 1964, p. 59.
22. A. Mansbridge. *An Adventure in Working-Class Education*, Longmans, 1920, p. 10.
23. Quoted from Leonard Clark, ed. *The Kingdom of the Mind, Essays and Addresses 1903–1937 of Albert Mansbridge*. Dent, 1944, p. 11.
24. Quoted from T. W. Price. *The Story of the Workers' Educational Association 1903–1924*. The Labour Publishing Company, 1924, p. 14.
25. *A History of Adult Education* . . ., Kelly, p. 249.
26. Arthur Bryant. *English Saga 1840–1940* (Collins, 1940) Fontana edn., p. 288.
27. *Civic Universities*, p. 236.

Part Two

Period of Incubation

4

False Dawn: 1918–25

Where war demands of all equal sacrifices, it was felt that to all should be accorded, so far as might be, equal opportunities.

H. A. L. Fisher, President of the Board of Education 1916–1922.[1]

In 1914 the lights went out all over Europe. But, as is well known, in modern times a major war has invariably provoked urgent demand for social reform; and almost invariably education has been put in the foreground of that demand.

During the early months of the First World War humane men and women in Britain grew shocked at the way in which selfish and unscrupulous employers, under the patriotic pretence of going all out in aid of the war effort, were ruthlessly exploiting the enthusiasm and energy of young employeees, in some cases overdriving them to the serious detriment of their health. By 1915 the Government felt obliged to take notice of the widespread concern. It set up a departmental committee, under the chairmanship of Herbert Lewis, M.P., Parliamentary Secretary to the Board of Education, 'to consider what steps should be taken to make provision for the education and instruction of children and young persons after the war'. The Committee was requested to pay particular regard to those who had been 'abnormally employed during the war'. In its Final Report, issued in April 1917 (one of the blacker periods of the war), the Lewis Committee offered, along with others, the following important recommendations:

1. That it be an obligation on the local education authority in each area to provide suitable continuation classes for young persons between the ages of 14 and 18 . . .
2. That it be an obligation upon all young persons between the ages of 14 and 18 to attend such day continuation classes . . .

The dry precision of these recommendations was vividly illuminated by the passage in the Report justifying them. 'Can the age of adolescence be brought out of the purview of economic exploitation and into that of the social conscience? Can the conception of the juvenile as primarily a little wage-earner be replaced by the conception of the juvenile as primarily the workman and the citizen in training?'

To do precisely that was a principal purpose of the Education Bill introduced into the House of Commons in 1917 by H. A. L. Fisher, lately Vice-Chancellor of Sheffield University, and the only practising educator ever made President of the Board of Education.

The time seemed propitious. As Fisher himself long after wrote:[2]

The country was in a spending mood and eager to compensate the wastage of war by some real contribution to the arts of peace ... the educational world was in a state of ferment. For the first time in our national history education was a popular subject and discussed in an atmosphere cleared of religious acrimony.

Fisher realized that this might be but a fleeting mood, that: 'While the war lasted reforms could be obtained and advances could be made which it would be impossible to realize in the critical atmosphere of peace.'[3] He decided, therefore, 'to move forward at a hand gallop and along the whole front'. Early in 1917 he got the Cabinet to accept in principle his programme. In the summer he introduced an Education Bill 'abolishing half-time, curtailing the industrial labour of school children, introducing compulsory part-time continuation schools, and generally enlarging the powers of the local authorities to promote every type of education from the nursery school upwards'.[4] The Bill was given a second reading before Parliament rose for the summer recess.

Having thus made the country aware of what he (and the Government) had in mind, Fisher spent the recess in testing public reactions to his proposals. He met with considerable criticism of those affecting the employment of children, especially in Lancashire and Yorkshire, the last strongholds of the 'half-time' system. Under this system children as young as thirteen spent the morning or the afternoon only at school, and during the other part of the day worked up to six hours in mill or factory. (I sat alongside 'half-timers' in a Yorkshire elementary school, and have never ceased to be grateful to our woman class teacher, who would not wake them up when they fell asleep during lessons. Her action—or inaction!—required some courage in the early years of the twentieth century.)

Fisher also met with the most moving support. His experience at Bristol, where he addressed 'a meeting of dockers, got together at a moment's notice by E. Bevin on a Sunday morning',[5] has been often quoted, but is well worth quoting once again.

> I have never encountered such enthusiasm. They did what I have never seen before or since, rose to their feet two or three times in the course of my speech, waved their handkerchiefs, and cheered themselves hoarse. The prospect of wider opportunities which the new plan for education might open to the disinherited filled them with enthusiasm.[6]

But Fisher was a realist. His next words offer a salutary warning to the overoptimistic: 'Alas! for these good folk. They expected from an Education Bill what no bill on education or on anything else can give, a new Heaven and a new Earth.'

Fisher had need of all his realism. He was made painfully aware that, as he said, 'It is always dangerous to interfere with vested interests.' First, his proposal to 'group local authorities in larger units' was met with a storm of protest. He gave in. 'I bowed to the storm. The measure was carefully stripped of every feature which might make it obnoxious to the public bodies [i.e. the local authorities] who would be required to work it.'[7]

Secondly, he was forced by the hostility of Lancashire MPs to restrict his scheme for day continuation schools by postponing for seven years its application to young people over sixteen. Even so, when the Education Act 1918 had become the law of the land, the day continuation scheme—much the most important *educational* item in the Act—crashed in ruin after only a few months; a resounding failure not yet—half a century later—made good, despite the re-enactment of the day continuation school clauses in the Education Act of 1944.

1918 reforms

But Fisher's Education Act was far from being a dead loss. On the contrary, it effected a round half-dozen permanent reforms of great value. It fixed the upper limit of 'compulsory school age' at fourteen for all, abolishing exemptions at an earlier age for any employment, however allegedly 'beneficial'; and thus ended—after three-quarters of a century—the 'half-time' system. It prohibited all employment of children under twelve, and restricted the employment of those between twelve and fourteen to a maximum of two hours a day. It prohibited the employment of children of school age in factories, mines, or street trading. (So the boy selling newspapers at the street corner, a familiar sight—and sound!—in my childhood days, dis-appeared overnight, at any rate officially. So did the little shoeblack and the child crossing sweeper.)

The Act ended the last vestiges of fee-charging in public elementary schools. It gave the LEAs statutory powers to raise the school-leaving age to fifteen in their areas and to establish and maintain nursery schools and classes for children under five—powers of which regret-tably few LEAs availed themselves. Nor can it be said that LEAs in general—there were some notable exceptions—made generous use of the powers given them to award maintenance grants to scholarship pupils in secondary schools; or of those which enabled them to pro-vide, or assist the provision of, swimming baths, holiday camps, or other facilities for physical training and games.

Finally, the Act introduced a system of percentage grants from the Government in aid of approved local authority expenditure. Fisher regarded this reform as of critical importance, because, in his opinion: 'The cause which had been arresting educational progress in the country was lack of financial support. . . . Too great a burden was borne by the rates, too small a proportion by the taxes.'[8] His principal reason for introducing percentage grants was to improve the salaries of elementary school teachers. Possibly his optimistic belief that, 'the change worked its expected magic' was shortlived, but the ending of the magic was due to economic factors beyond his control. At the time, as he records, 'the average wage of the teacher in an elementary school was doubled'.[9]

A quarter of a century later, a Government White Paper warned[10] that 'Legislation can do little more than prepare the way for reform'. Until an Act of Parliament is implemented it remains a mere gesture. The major tragedy of the 1918 Act, the collapse of the day continua-tion school clauses, remains a continuing discredit to our country. But in addition several other highly important sections of the Act were either scarcely implemented at all or much less so than they should have been. The slight use made by most LEAs of valuable permissive powers granted to them must have been peculiarly disappointing to Fisher. One of his chief ambitions had been, in the words of the late Dr S. J. Curtis, 'to place the onus of reconstruction on the local authorities and to rely on their public spirit and initiative to carry through the proposals [of the Education Act] in the way that was intended'.[11]

The failure of many LEAs to rise to the height of Fisher's challenge is yet another illustration of the unhappy fact that, unless there is some powerful inducement, local authorities tend to be lukewarm in their attitude towards the use of permissive powers. In the years immediately following the First World War they had plenty of excuses, if no good reason. Financial crises followed one another in rapid succession. By 1921 there were over two million unemployed, and an unknown, but certainly large, number of children existing on, at best, one square meal a day. I met many while teaching in the West Riding from 1922 to 1925. The enthusiasm for education manifested by Ernest Bevin's dockers, and many other sections of the public, all too quickly died away. Far too many ratepayers remained reluctant to pay out much for public education and far too many town and county councillors got elected by promising they would not have to.

Reluctance was even extended to the performance of statutory duties. Section 2(1)(a) of the 1918 Act *required* LEAs (i.e. made it their duty) to provide in public elementary schools, by means of central schools or classes, or otherwise: (i) practical instruction suitable to the ages, abilities, and requirements of the children, and (ii) courses of advanced instruction for the older or more intelligent pupils. Some authorities had done this for years. The London County Council had launched in 1910 a system of central schools which provided a four-year course, from eleven to fifteen, for elementary school pupils who expected to enter employment direct from school, and who desired a vocationally biased post-primary curriculum. Manchester started a similar scheme about a year later. A few LEAs, mainly in the north of England, followed their example. But, despite the fact that it was a duty, most had done little and many nothing at all. When in 1925 'the Board of Education made an inquiry into the number of authorities and schools "giving advanced instruction of the sort contemplated in Section 20 of the Education Act 1921"' they found that while 158 LEAs claimed to be making such provision, most of them were in fact doing precious little. The average number of senior elementary departments per LEA giving advanced instruction was under five, and 'the number of children in advanced courses formed only 5·4 per cent of the total number of children over 11 attending the public elementary schools'.[12] Nevertheless, slight though this provision was, it had an important impact on the future of secondary education in England and Wales, for its value greatly impressed the Board of Education's Consultative Committee, then engaged on the investigations which led to the seminal report on *The Education of the Adolescent*.

It is obvious . . . that both the facility with which an advanced course can be planned, as a systematic whole, and its value to the pupil, will be greatly increased if the school life lasts for four years

7

after the age of 11. It is not less obvious . . . that the disposition to remain at school will be strengthened by any arrangement of the curriculum which causes the pupil and his parents to feel that, far from retraversing again ground already covered, he is beginning a new and vital part of his school career. [13]

Burnham scales

Fisher followed up his reform of the grant system by securing a revolutionary improvement in the arrangements for paying teachers. The existing arrangements were chaotic. Each LEA made its own; consequently, salaries varied enormously over the country—and so, naturally, did the quality of the teachers employed. During the war the cost of living rose sharply, but the average amount of teachers' salaries did not. In 1917, as a temporary expedient, Fisher arranged a supplementary grant of over £300,000. At the same time he appointed a departmental committee, under the chairmanship of Viscount Burnham, and including representatives of the LEAs' and teachers' associations, to investigate the principles on which teachers' salaries should be based.

The committee recommended that salaries should be fixed nationally, by agreements negotiated between the LEAs as the employers, and teachers' associations as representing the employees. Fisher accepted the recommendation, and in September, 1919, established the first Burnham Committee: a standing committee of the Board of Education constituted for the purpose of negotiating national salary scales for teachers in public elementary schools. It consisted of two panels, representing respectively the LEAs and the teachers, with a neutral chairman. The procedure it evolved was that each panel in turn scrutinized proposals made by the other until agreement was reached. There were (after the first few months) no 'round table' discussions; the panels met separately, and agreed their proposals, which were then presented by the leaders. Only the panel leaders spoke in plenary session.

Similar committees, also under Lord Burnham's chairmanship, were shortly afterwards established for maintained secondary schools and technical colleges. All three committees agreed salary scales which came into operation in September 1921. These first scales were not, in view of the rise in the cost of living, overgenerous, and within twelve months the 'Geddes axe' (the Committee on National Expenditure, chaired by Sir Eric Geddes) chopped 5 per cent off them; but it was the principles on which they were based that mattered: that salaries should be freely negotiated between employers and employed, that the Exchequer and the local rates should bear fixed proportions of the cost, and that the scales should be effective nationally. Unfortunately, the last principle was carried out in practice in a most invidious manner. There were different salary scales for technical, secondary, and elementary teachers—the last being, needless to say, the lowest—and for elementary school teachers there were three standard scales for different types of area throughout the country, and a fourth obtainable only in the Metropolitan area. Nevertheless, the Burnham scales, with all their anomalies, were an immense improvement on the previous 'catch as catch can' competition between LEAs.

In 1918 Fisher tackled also the matter of teachers' pensions, until then very inadequately provided for. His Superannuation Act, passed in the autumn of that year, was a most generous measure. It extended to all teachers in maintained and grant-aided schools and colleges (except university colleges) a non-contributory pension scheme. But the sequel was as sad as it was swift. The Geddes committee pounced on the non-contributory aspect, denounced it as an example of official extravagance, and recommended that the scheme be made a contributory one. The Government agreed—and teachers found 5 per cent being deducted from their salaries. They have neither forgotten nor forgiven what they regarded, not without reason, as a gross breach of faith on the part of the Government.

Education for adults

Both the Education Act and the Teachers' Superannuation Act were passed before the end of the 1914–18 war. They epitomized the spirit of exaltation and optimism in which Britain emerged from the war that was to 'end all wars' and 'make the world safe for democracy'. This spirit expressed itself in a passionate desire (felt only, alas! by some sections of society) to increase largely all forms of social opportunity hitherto reserved to the more privileged classes. The purpose of the 1918 Education Act, for example, was explicitly stated, in its first clause, to be 'the establishment of a national system of public education available for all persons capable of profiting thereby'. Not only social justice was felt to be involved; it was also essential to make the country industrially efficient. The war had exposed with stark cruelty how lamentably inefficient were many parts of its industrial machinery. To achieve either of these aims it was necessary, as Fisher said when introducing his Education Bill,[14] to 'assume that education should be the education of the whole man, spiritually, intellectually, and physically'. He felt confident that it was possible to devise a scheme of education 'from which the whole youth of the country, male and female, may derive benefit.'

The need for such education was not restricted only to the young. Some of the ablest minds in Britain—they included R. H. Tawney, A. L. Smith, then Master of Balliol College, Oxford, and William Temple, a future Archbishop of Canterbury—realized, first, that it was equally necessary for older persons, especially those who had not been able to secure it in their youth, and secondly, that to make any system of adult education purely vocational would be unwise, even perhaps dangerous. These views were expressed in one of the most perceptive (but least read) official Reports on education ever compiled in England, that of the Adult Education Committee of the Ministry of Reconstruction, published in 1919. In presenting the Report to the Prime Minister, Mr Lloyd George, the Master of Balliol, as Chairman, wrote that his committee had come to the 'necessary conclusion' that:

> adult education [i.e. non-vocational education for adults] must not be regarded as a luxury for a few exceptional persons here and there, nor as a thing which concerns only a short span of early manhood, but that adult education is a permanent national necessity, an inseparable aspect of citizenship, and therefore should be both universal and lifelong.

Brave, and true, words—whose promise was, like so much else of good proposed in these years, to be quickly blighted by the arctic winds of national 'economy'. Yet even in the persistently neglected field of non-vocational adult education some gains were made.

'When sufficient time has elapsed', said the Final Report of the Adult Education Committee of the Ministry of Reconstruction in November 1919, 'to enable the events of the war to be seen in their true perspective, the rise and development of the educational movement among the armed forces will stand out as one of the most striking and unpredictable.' 'That, I think, is now recognized', wrote Lord Gorell[15] towards the end of his life. With some pride, no doubt, for it was he who during the summer of 1918 singlehanded drafted a new scheme for Army education which forty years later was still regarded by those who directed it as 'part of the national system'. And no one would deny that there was some advance in civilian adult education; but when I recall what many of us, young soldiers returned from the war, dreamed and discussed, and contrast that with what actually happened...

Vocational education fared better; it is so much easier to appreciate the short-term, and measurable, results of specific training for employment. After twenty-one years of abstention, the Government began again to make grants in aid of capital expenditure on technical colleges. Also, in response to a widespread feeling that the existing regional examinations in technical subjects needed to be supplemented by a system of national awards, the Board of Education and the Institution of Mechanical Engineers jointly launched in 1921 a scheme of National Certificates and Diplomas in that branch of engineering. Diplomas could be gained only by full-time study, certificates only by part-time. It was a condition of entry to a certificate course that the student should be in full-time employment in an occupation to which his course was relevant. Both certificates and diplomas were available at two levels, Ordinary (ONC and OND), and Higher (HNC and HND). The certificates were popular from the start. During the next few years several more schemes were started; chemistry (1922), electrical engineering (1923), naval architecture (1927), building (1930). This was one of the few innovations which survived the recurrent economy freezes between the wars. It must be added, however, that popular as were the certificates, the drop-out rate was high. This is almost inevitable with any scheme which superimposes serious and sustained theoretical studies upon full-time employment; and it took a minimum of three years to secure an ONC, five to get HNC. Diplomas attracted relatively very few students; the idea of full-time technical education had not yet penetrated the English mind.

The 1914–18 war almost emptied the universities of male students and younger members of the academic staff. But it set in train developments that were to prove of the utmost importance for the future of British universities. The earliest of these was the creation in 1915 of the Department of Scientific and Industrial Research (DSIR), which was called into being because of the manifest shortage of research workers in almost every field of science and technology. DSIR benefited the universities in two ways; first because it was clearly their business to train a large proportion of the research workers needed, and secondly because it was assumed that a great deal of the research which DSIR would sponsor would be undertaken in universities and university colleges.

Universities in the red

A second important development was that in 1916 the Committee responsible for assessing the universities' financial needs and advising the Government what grants to make, which since 1907 had been reporting to the Board of Education (greatly to the universities' disgust), was transferred back to the Treasury. This was regarded as recognition of the universities' right to greater freedom of action than was allowable to institutions within the statutory system of public education. The impression was confirmed in 1919, when a permanent University Grants Committee (UGC) was created (its predecessors were temporary phenomena) and made a statutory committee of the Treasury. The new committee was given two specific functions, (i) to inquire into the financial needs of university education in the United Kingdom, and (ii) to advise the Government as to the application of any grants that may be made by Parliament towards meeting them.

The UGC was also among the innovations which survived the post-war economic crises—to become later a piece of machinery which excited admiration throughout the Western world. But it is essential to realize how limited in 1919, and for long after, were its ambit and its powers. In 1908 and 1909 two principles had been laid down as governing state aid to British Universities.

1. The main object of Treasury grants is maintenance rather than initial or capital expenditure.
2. State aid to university teaching would be of doubtful advantage if it did not stimulate private effort and induce benefactors to contribute in the present day as they did in the olden times.

The Treasury had adhered strictly to those principles, despite the fact that benefactors had not contributed 'as they did in the olden times'. Consequently, when in 1919 the Government launched a generous scholarship scheme for men and women from the armed and auxiliary services, the universities had to endure (that seems the only appropriate word) a boom for which their existing premises and, numerically, their academic staffs, were patently inadequate. Quite insufficient funds were made available to put things right. Admittedly, for a year or two after the war the Government showed itself uncharacteristically generous; it made grants for capital expenditure amounting to some £700,000, and it more than doubled the annual grants for recurrent expenditure, from about £275,000 to nearly £600,000 in 1920–1. But £700,000 did not go very far when divided among forty-five universities and university colleges, and the increase in the amount of recurrent grant barely kept pace with the increase in the number of full-time students, which was by 1920–1 more than double that of 1913–14: in England, 24,963 in place of 12,038. The purchasing power of the £ was not more than half of what it had been in pre-war days. Soon the universities and university colleges were financially in a sorry state. How badly off they were was revealed in the UGC Report for 1920–1.[16]

> Of the 45 Universities and Colleges which carry forward a balance on revenue account, 29 incurred deficits on the year's working—some of these deficits are very considerable . . . moreover, 25 Institutions show accumulated deficits as at July 31st, 1921; in some cases these amounts are very large.

Only twenty of the university institutions—fewer than half—had accumulated surpluses, and these, said the UGC, were 'with one or two exceptions . . . of moderate amount'. There were also instances of 'large debts on capital account'.

Somehow, the universities and colleges struggled on. Two factors, one mildly encouraging, the other anything but, enabled them to survive, if only at subsistence level. The annual Treasury grants for recurrent expenditure (though not for capital) continued to grow; by 1939 they exceeded £2 million. Secondly, after the postwar 'bulge' of ex-service men and women had worked itself out, no attempt was made to increase further the number of university students, despite the fact that secondary school pupils were knocking at university doors in ever growing numbers and with steadily improving academic qualifications. The number of full-time students actually dropped slightly during the 1930s. Admittedly, these were years of severe economic crises and massive unemployment; even so, it was craven policy to reduce the capacity of such powerhouses of intellectual ability, especially as their cost to the nation was no more than marginal.

'The scholarship'

The educational institution which remained fullest of vigorous life throughout the period between the wars was, without any doubt, the maintained secondary school—the grammar school as it is called today. From the earliest postwar years it was almost everywhere bursting at the seams, yet having to reject annually thousands of eager and able youngsters, most of whom had qualified for entry by winning scholarships or free places. The free-place examination—

predecessor of the 'eleven-plus'—had never been what it was originally intended to be, simply a qualifying test; it now became in numerous areas murderously competitive. Twenty candidates for one place was not unknown. Many secondary schools were so heavily oversubscribed that they had to reject also large numbers of would-be paying pupils.

The reasons for this universal popularity of the secondary school varied from district to district, but in many—probably the majority—could be summed up in one word: security. This was particularly the case in areas of heavy industry, such as the West Riding of Yorkshire, where I saw it at first hand during the years 1922–5. 'The scholarship', which secured one of the coveted free places in a secondary school, offered the best (if not the only) chance of escape from the terrifying insecurity of employment in the mining, engineering, and textile industries; and the rest of the family would, almost literally, starve themselves in order to maintain the bright boy at the secondary school. The prizes which this school—and no other—could offer were the School and Higher School Certificates, which had become the 'open sesame' to the safety and status of the clerical—the 'white collar'—occupations. And, for the few whose ambition was more vaulting, these certificates were the key that could unlock the door to the university, and so to the dizzy heights of a professional career.

The School and Higher School Certificates, awarded respectively on the results of the First and Second School Examinations, were instituted in (of all years!) 1917. But their origins go back to the fruitful decade immediately preceding the First World War. The new secondary schools had already become the happy hunting ground of a horde of examining bodies—at one time they numbered over fifty—and consequently of an increasing number of unhappy pupils, spoon-fed and crammed for the sole purpose of passing examinations. In 1909 the Board of Education, having failed to check the evil by direct action, referred the matter to its Consultative Committee. This made in 1911 [17] two critically important recommendations.

1. That presenting young and immature pupils for external examinations was a mischievous practice, and should be restrained; and
2. That the various examinations being offered to secondary schools should be coordinated.

As a result of protracted negotiations, further delayed by the onset of war, the seven university examining bodies agreed to remodel their schemes to fit into the proposed pattern of two examinations: the first, for the School Certificate, on a general curriculum, to be taken by pupils aged about sixteen (i.e. the age at which most pupils left the secondary school for employment); and the second, for the Higher School Certificate (HSC), taken approximately two years later, on a more specialized curriculum chosen from one of three groups of subjects: classics, modern languages, science and mathematics. To coordinate the syllabuses and standards of the examining bodies the Board of Education established in 1917 the Secondary School Examinations Council (SSEC), representative of the examining bodies, the teachers, and the LEAs, with a Chairman appointed by the Board of Education. It also made two extremely important announcements.

1. That it would offer a special grant of £400 a year for an 'advanced' (i.e. post-school certificate) course in secondary schools;
2. That it would recognize no external examination in grant-earning secondary schools below the standard of the School Certificate examination.

Given thus a monopoly in the schools, the certificates acquired enormous prestige in the eyes of parents, pupils, teachers, and employers alike. A School Certificate which included a sufficient number of appropriate passes at 'credit' level to exempt the holder from the necessity of sitting university entrance examinations (called 'matriculation' at London and other universities), soon became the necessary passport to professional and quasiprofessional occupations in which a start could be made at age 16–17. (Employers quickly grasped the fact that 'matric' meant something better than mere 'school cert.') The HSC as quickly became the necessary passport to a subsidized place at a university; particularly after 1920, when the Board of Education began to offer annually 200 'state scholarships', tenable at universities and other institutions of higher education, and awarded these on the results of the HSC examinations.

The growing demand of employers and professional associations for 'matric' inevitably led to more spoonfeeding and cramming in secondary schools. Quite a considerable proportion of candidates for the School Certificate got through the examination on their teacher's brains rather than their own, as I know to my personal discredit. Faced with a history class of delightful, but not highly intelligent and far from hardworking fifth formers who I knew would never pass on their own ability and efforts, I supplied them with model answers, which I bade them memorize; and I bet them that these would cover a sufficient number of the questions they would meet to guarantee them a pass. I won my bet. They came out of the examination room grinning like monkeys. They all passed.

The School Certificate undoubtedly lent itself to such sharp practice. Another weakness in it was that when it was made a 'grouped' examination, one of the four groups of subjects, the one comprising the fine arts and handicrafts, was given an inferior status to the others; results in that group did not contribute either to a pass in the examination or to any exemption a candidate might desire. Consequently art, music, and handicrafts tended to be neglected in secondary schools, especially boys' schools, in favour of the more academic subjects.

These and other defects were ultimately to kill the School Certificate. On the other hand it must be recorded that during the early years after the First World War the two certificate examinations, but particularly the School Certificate, which directly affected the work of much the larger number of pupils, had a bracing, and beneficial, effect upon the still young and immature statutory system of secondary education. They benefited both teachers and taught. They gave the schools precise academic targets; set what were at the time very high academic standards; compelled steady, sustained, systematic and disciplined work; and offered tangible, and relevant, rewards for success. Later, unfortunately, much of this became less true; but the impact of the certificates was never wholly bad.

I hope this chapter has made clear that the first half-dozen years or so after the 1914–18 war present a very mixed record. Many hopes were dashed, many enthusiasms chilled, many promising beginnings nipped in the bud. On the other hand, sound foundations were laid for a number of developments which later proved important and valuable. For those teachers who were longing for immediate revolutionary reform (I was one of them), these were years of perpetual frustration, evoking at times feelings of furious despair. Perhaps it is recollection of those feelings which prompted me to entitle this chapter 'False Dawn'. The period was undoubtedly the beginning of a new era—but so much of the enlightenment it promised had to be (or at any rate was) deferred.

Notes

1. *An Unfinished Autobiography*, Oxford University Press, 1940, p. 94.
2. *Ibid.*
3. *Ibid.*, p. 103.
4. *Ibid.*, p. 106.
5. *Ibid.*
6. *Ibid.*, pp. 106–7.
7. *Ibid.*, p. 107.

8. *Ibid.*, p. 104.
9. *Ibid.*
10. *Educational Reconstruction*, 1943, p. 26.
11. *History of Education in Great Britain*, 2nd edn., University Tutorial Press, 1950, p. 341.
12. Report of the Consultative Committee of the Board of Education on *The Education of the Adolescent*, HMSO, 1926, pp. 48–9. (The 1918 Education Act was absorbed into the 1921 Act, a consolidating Act which brought together all previous educational legislation.)
13. *Ibid.*, p. 49.
14. 10 August 1917, Hansard, xcvii, col. 814.
15. In his autobiography *One Man ... Many Parts*, Odhams Press, 1956, p. 207.
16. *Returns from Universities and University Colleges in Receipt of Treasury Grant*, 1920–21, Section 9.
17. *Report of the Consultative Committee of the Board of Education on Examinations in Secondary Schools*, chap. v.

5

Thinking Aloud

*We desire to abolish the word 'elementary', and to alter and extend the sense
of the word 'secondary'. The word 'elementary' has now become misleading
. . . We propose to substitute the term 'primary', but to restrict the use of that
term to the period of education which ends at the age of eleven or twelve. To
the period of education which follows upon it we would give the name
secondary; and we would make this name embrace all forms of post-primary
education . . .*

Report of the Consultative Committee of the Board of Education
on *The Education of the Adolescent.*[1]

During the earlier years of the 1914–18 war there was considerable
public agitation in favour of 'secondary education for all'. This was
led, on the left by R. H. Tawney, the Labour Party's spokesman on
educational policy, and on the right (or at least much nearer the
centre) by *The Times Educational Supplement*, then in the vigorous first
flush of its lusty youth. (It was born in 1910.) The *Supplement*, in a
leading article on 5 October 1915, said:

> In our view the problem of the elimination of human waste and the
> multiplication of human efficiency can only be secured by a uni-
> versal system of secondary education. . . . There should be . . .
> preparatory education up to the age of eleven years . . . and from
> that age onwards there should be in every school in the land com-
> pulsory secondary education for every child. . . . The scholarship
> and bursary system has nothing to recommend it. It turns certain
> elementary schools into cramming shops for scholarships; it never
> effectively reaches the great reserves of intelligence and genius that
> are part of all schools alike.

Pretty strong stuff that to come from a newspaper widely regarded—
despite its acquisition by Lord Northcliffe—as a pillar of the Establishment. Admittedly, the *Supplement* was shortly afterwards to be con-

verted by the Report of the Lewis Committee to 'the ideal of universal apprenticeship'. Some sections of the Labour Party were similarly converted, at least for the time being; but not Tawney and those who thought with him. In a seminal book published in 1922 on behalf of the Education Advisory Committee of the Labour Party Tawney wrote that:

> The Labour Party is convinced that the only policy which is at once educationally sound and suited to a democratic community is one under which primary education and secondary education are organized as two stages in a single and continuous process; secondary education being the education of the adolescent and primary education being education preparatory thereto. *Its objective, therefore, is both the improvement of primary education and the development of public secondary education to such a point that all normal children, irrespective of the income, class or occupation of their parents, may be transferred at the age of eleven + from the primary or preparatory school to one type or another of secondary school, and remain in the latter till sixteen.*[2]

The Hadow Reports

Strikingly similar proposals were made four years later in the first of the three great Hadow Reports produced by the Board of Education's Consultative Committee, that on *The Education of the Adolescent*, published in December 1926. But this is not at all surprising, since Tawney was a member of that Committee, and according to all accounts (except his own) its leading spirit. This gives a measure of his stature, for the group of people assembled to advise Sir Charles Trevelyan, first Labour President of the Board of Education, about courses of study suitable for children remaining at school until fifteen in schools other than secondary (i.e. grammar) schools was as variously eminent as any Minister could desire. It included the historian Ernest Barker, the statesman Lord Gorell, the founder of the WEA, Albert Mansbridge, two distinguished heads of public schools, Miss E. M. Tanner (Roedean) and W. W. Vaughan (Rugby), and two equally distinguished heads of training colleges, Miss Lynda Grier and Miss Freda Hawtrey.

The recommendations made in *The Education of the Adolescent* are set out at length in every general history of English education, and the Report itself is widely accessible. They will not, therefore, be summarized here. The crucial recommendations are those in the passage quoted at the head of this chapter. It is these which give the Report its outstanding importance. The rest, a curious mixture of progressive

99

and traditional thinking, are either directly ancillary to them or compromises hopefully offered as adjustments to the circumstances of the times.

Few official reports on English education can have received a warmer or more widespread welcome. To some of us school teachers *The Education of the Adolescent* was for a while hardly less than holy writ. Few reports have had more profound impact upon our educational history. But though its basic principles still stand as firm as ever—that education is a continuous process to be conducted in progressive stages, and that a humane and liberal education can be given by other means than books alone—not much else of what it proposed is left intact today. Most of its suggested structure for secondary education—selective and non-selective central schools, central departments, senior schools and classes, 'higher tops'—was demolished in 1944. Within another quarter of a century the country was getting rid of the principal institution which resulted from the 1944 Act, the secondary modern school, and with it Hadow's proposed bipartite organization of secondary education.

This is not to belittle the Report on *The Education of the Adolescent*. But it was not, as it has been so often described, a revolutionary document far ahead of its time. (Had it been, it would not have been nearly so well received as it was.) It was a synthesis of current progressive thought and practice (of a not too advanced nature) with a great many ideas and much practice that were conventional almost to the point of obsolescence. It was far behind the thought of some of the educational pioneers of the early 1920s, and considerably behind the practice of the most progressive LEAs, and of many teachers in maintained as well as independent schools. As the Report shows (pp. 57–64), a number of LEAs were already carrying out what later became known as 'Hadow reorganization'. In some areas, e.g. Leicester, this was far advanced.

The Education of the Adolescent was published only a few months after Britain's one and only General Strike. Before that, there had been during the years following the war many other strikes, and two severe financial crises. The Board of Education, well aware of the country's unstable economy, welcomed the Hadow Report warmly in principle, but coolly in practice. It took serious note of considerations which we enthusiastic young teachers were apt to ignore or dismiss airily: that, for example, to raise the school leaving age to fifteen—advocated by Hadow (para. 168) as 'the course of wisdom'—would require the provision of 350,000 additional school places and at least 12,000 more teachers. And that many people thought other needs more urgent than raising the school age; reducing the number and size of over-large classes, for instance, or improving voluntary school buildings, still many of them in a shocking state. Instead of attempting impossibilities, the Board advised,[3] go for the other, easier (and cheaper) reform Hadow had recommended: the division of the all-age elementary school into two schools, primary and senior. Much of that could be accomplished by the expenditure of only marginal sums of money.

The Board's advice was followed—except during the disastrous two years (1929–31) when the second Labour Government attempted, unsuccessfully, to raise the school leaving age. Before and after that period, despite the unprecedented economic crisis of 1931–3, which halted all but the most essential new school building, 'Hadow reorganization' of the elementary school jogged on, unhurriedly, and probably for that reason without much friction in most areas. There was a certain amount of outcry in some of the villages whose schools were 'decapitated', that is, had their pupils over eleven transferred to other schools. But generally this soon died down, especially where the senior boys and girls were able to return home at night with glowing stories of the equipment and activities of the 'modern' school to which they had been transferred.

Forty years or more after the event, I am prepared to defend the Board's policy—against which I protested as loudly as anyone at the time. I would defend it, not on the grounds on which it was then defended, but on purely educational grounds: that the leisurely progress of Hadow reorganization gave teachers time to learn, and to like, new ways of dealing with the 'juniors' in the primary school, and with adolescent boys and girls of modest intellectual ability in the 'modern' and 'senior' elementary schools. Many of us discovered in those days, as many teachers have discovered since, that given appropriate curricula and methods such girls and boys will rise to unexpected heights in work, play and behaviour.

'Activity and experience'

Much amazingly good experimental work was done between 1926 and 1939 in senior elementary schools, especially perhaps in girls' schools. (The pity of it is that most of it has not been, and probably never will be, put on record.) But I am inclined to believe that the most substantial educational advance during these years was made by the junior school. I have always considered that the 1931 Hadow Report, entitled *The Primary School* but dealing almost exclusively with the education of Juniors (that is, pre-adolescent children between the ages of 7–8 and 11–12), is every whit as good as *The Education of the Adolescent*, and may have proved in the long run even more beneficial to the country's children. The *Education of the Adolescent* dealt largely with the structure of the educational system (though it contained two good chapters on the curriculum), but *The Primary School* concentrated upon telling teachers, (i) what pre-adolescent children were really like (and its psychology was sounder than that of the 1926 Report); and (ii) exactly, and in great detail, what they should try to do with them in school.[4] Not *for* them, but *along with* them, and with their active involvement and co-operation. Their curriculum, said the Committee (para. 75), 'is to be thought of in terms of activity and experience rather than of knowledge to be acquired and facts to be stored', because:

> At the age when they attend the primary [i.e. junior] schools, children are active and inquisitive, delighting in movement, in small tasks that they can perform with deftness and skill, and in the sense of visible and tangible accomplishment which such tasks offer; intensely interested in the character and purpose—the shape, form, colour and use—of the material objects around them; at once absorbed in creating their own miniature world of imagination and emotion, and keen observers who take pleasure in reproducing their observations by speech and dramatic action; and still engaged in mastering a difficult and unfamiliar language, without knowing that they are doing so, because it is a means of communicating with other human beings (Introduction, p. xvii).

'These activities are not aimless', declared the Committee. They 'form the process by which children grow' and 'are, in a very real sense, their education'. Unhappily, a great deal of foolishness was committed by unwise or inexperienced teachers who misinterpreted the Committee's dictum about 'activity and experience'; who took it to mean any activity, however pointless, and any experience, good, bad, or indifferent; and who thereby brought 'activity methods' into a quite undeserved disrepute. What such teachers omitted to do was to 'read, mark, learn, and inwardly digest' the sentences in which the Committee went on to explain the purpose of a curriculum 'thought of in terms of activity and experience'.

> Its aim should be to develop in a child the fundamental human powers and to awaken him to the fundamental interests of civilized life so far as these powers and interests lie within the compass of childhood, to encourage him to attain gradually to that control and

orderly management of his energies, impulses and emotions, which is the essence of moral and intellectual discipline, to help him to discover the idea of duty and to ensue it, and to open out his imagination and his sympathies in such a way that he may be prepared to understand and to follow in later years the highest examples of excellence in life and conduct (Report, para. 75).

They did great harm, those teachers, with their classrooms full of chaotic noise and movement: a harm out of all proportion to their numbers, for they were never more than a small minority. A vastly greater host of junior school teachers have, from the day the 1931 Report was published down to the present time, set themselves patiently and intelligently to put into practice the precepts of that Report. With great and increasing success, so that at its best Junior School teaching and learning is today at least as good as any in the entire spectrum of English education.

The third Report in the magnificent Hadow trilogy, on *Infant and Nursery Schools*, which was published in 1933, also concentrated on the physical and mental make-up of young children, and on the educational programme and the methods that teachers should use, rather than on the structure and organization of schools. But in this case it was recapitulation of already established excellences, not revelation of what might be, as in the case of the junior school. The infants' school had a tradition of enlightenment going back over one hundred years to Robert Owen, David Stow, Samuel Wilderspin and a score of other pioneers; a tradition kept vigorously alive throughout the nineteenth century by the Pestalozzians of the Home and Colonial Infant School Society and the English disciples of Friedrich Froebel; a tradition given new life and new means of expression in the twentieth century by Margaret and Rachel McMillan, Maria Montessori, and the leaders of the new Froebel movement. The junior school had no tradition save that of being the least considered part of the public elementary school. *The Primary School* report preached what was to most teachers an entirely new gospel; and to their eternal credit great numbers of them set out eagerly to learn it. Had they not been handicapped by the necessity, due largely to parental pressure, of preparing their intellectually most able pupils for 'the scholarship' their success would have been even more resounding.

In terms of obvious large-scale advance the 1920s and 1930s have by comparison with the first decade of the twentieth century relatively little to offer. Much of their record is, unhappily, of recurrent setbacks, frustrations, and outright failures: the dropping of the day

8

continuation school scheme; the savaging of teachers' material prospects by the Geddes and May Reports; the repeated failure to raise the school leaving age; the stillborn compromise of the 1936 Education Act (which would have revived the barbarous nineteenth-century practice of exempting children from school for what was euphemistically termed 'beneficial employment'); the exasperatingly slow progress of 'Hadow reorganization' in many rural districts, and among church schools; the virtual cessation of new school building between 1931 and 1936; the concurrent serious unemployment among teachers, due partly to financial stringency, partly to falling school rolls; the near collapse of a number of voluntary training colleges which had enlarged their premises and increased the number of their students in anticipation of the expected raising of the school leaving age, and were left with empty places and large debts when it failed to materialize; the failure of the first President of the Board of Education genuinely interested in technical education, Lord Eustace Percy, to communicate his enthusiasm to an apathetic people; and finally the fateful 1 September 1939, when once again the lights went out all over Europe.

If, however, one looks at the years between the wars as a period in which ideas were being conceived and born and nurtured experimentally into tentative practice, it is possible to regard them as being much more fruitful than the foregoing paragraphs would seem to suggest. The titles I have given to this part of my book, 'Period of Incubation' and this chapter, 'Thinking Aloud', are (like most titles) gross oversimplifications, but I chose them to emphasize my conviction that the apparently barren years between the wars did a great deal to make possible the massive educational reforms which were so readily accepted by public opinion during the Second World War, and so unquestioningly incorporated in the Education Act of 1944. I believe that those reforms, and that Act, would not have received anything like so universal, and certainly not so rapturous, a welcome had not the principles and the ideas on which they were based been patiently and perseveringly shaped and developed by school teachers and educational administrators in all parts of the country during the years between 1918 and 1939. The rest of this chapter is devoted to a brief documentation of that belief.

Training of teachers

The 1925 *Report of the Departmental Committee on the Training of Teachers for Public Elementary Schools*, and the changes to which it led in the system of teacher training, may be regarded, according to taste, either as one of the crops planted during these years which were later to produce a rich harvest, or as one of the illustrations of frustrating failure. In my opinion, they contained elements of both.

Frustration was clearly manifest in the Report itself; of the eighteen members of the Committee, four refused to sign it, and four others refused to accept some of its recommendations and wrote stiff notes of dissent or reservation. Of the principal recommendations which were agreed by the majority of the Committee, one remained unfulfilled for forty-five years: 'That evidence of the successful completion of an approved course of training should be required as condition of recognition as a teacher . . .' Admittedly, this requirement was demanded only in respect of a teacher 'in a Public Elementary school', but we cannot take any comfort from that. It has been a deplorable defect in our educational system that men and women who have never undergone a single hour of professional training have been officially rated, and paid, as qualified teachers on the strength of having scraped through the examination for a first degree.

Some of the Committee's recommendations—the abolition of the Acting Teacher's Certificate, for example—are now of historical interest only, as reminders of 'old, unhappy, far-off times'. The recommendation most pregnant with promise of fruitful development was that:

> . . . in order to link the training colleges more closely with the universities, Joint Examining Bodies should be established, representative of universities and of the governing bodies of colleges, to examine [training college] students . . . for the purpose of the recognition of the students by the Board [of Education] as Certificated Teachers.

This recommendation went some way towards meeting the colleges' long-felt desire for closer professional links with the universities. Its importance lay in the fact that it involved a significant transfer of control in the field of teacher training. It meant, in short, that the Board of Education should cease to examine training college students for the Teacher's Certificate, and should hand over this function to the colleges themselves in cooperation with the universities. But the Board and its predecessor, the Committee of the Privy Council on Education, had conducted the examinations for the Teacher's Certificate so long as teacher training colleges in the modern sense had existed in England and Wales; and the power this gave to determine the academic and professional studies and standards of the country's future teachers was not one to be lightly given up. Admittedly, since 1890 the Education Department had accepted the results of university examinations in academic subjects as exempting training college students from Part II of its Certificate examination; but it had never relinquished hold of the professional subjects or of teaching practice.

The transfer was made—though the Board of Education continued to examine the practical teaching. The Joint Examining Bodies—or Joint Boards as they came to be known—took over in 1929 and 1930. There were ten of them; nine covering England, and one for Wales. Some seem to have done their job well, or at least well enough to make half of the McNair Committee, fifteen years later, wish to see the Joint Board system continued in only a slightly amended form. Some, on the other hand, justified the criticism made by the other half of the McNair Committee, that the Joint Board scheme had not produced the results hoped for when it was planned; had not brought training colleges and university institutions into any constitutional relationship; had not breached the iron curtain between training colleges and university training departments; had not—most damning criticism of all—even 'promoted among the training colleges themselves any more intimate relationship than they had twenty years ago',[5] at any rate 'so far as the pooling of staff and sharing of facilities are concerned'. Looking back, one wonders how the Joint Boards, hampered by their limited remit, could have been expected to perform such miracles—especially during a period of acute financial, and academic, depression such as the first five years after they assumed their responsibilities, when the number of university students was dropping, when the numbers in training colleges and UTDs were being reduced by governmental edict year after year, when the very existence of some colleges was threatened, and when mounting unemployment among certificated and graduate teachers alike was adding to the general gloom.

Towards a new order

Organizational and administrative changes in educational systems are easy to document; with the imponderables of ethos, atmosphere, aims, attitudes, objectives, and even with the less elusive matters of curricula, syllabuses, and methods, it is much more difficult to be precise. There are, however, means of making rough and ready assessments. One is to take note of the trend and tone of contemporary speeches and writings. Those of the later 1930s generally indicate a belief that profoundly important changes for the better were taking place. Here are three examples. In 1935, not in any respect a particularly remarkable year (though the economic clouds were certainly lifting), the President of the Board of Education, Oliver Stanley, declared that 'we have been witnessing a change of attitude and outlook in education comparable only to that change which took place in the fourteenth and fifteenth centuries and which we generally describe as the Renaissance'. One is naturally tempted to dismiss such an utterance as merely an example of the rhetorical exaggeration dear to politicians' hearts. But when one discovers so sober and reliable an educational historian as Charles Birchenough stating in cold print only a year or two later that 'if the difference in the education represented by the editions of 1905 and 1927 [of the *Handbook of Suggestions for Teachers*] is striking, that between 1905 and 1937 is so great as to constitute a new order',[6] it becomes no longer possible to regard such claims as the effervescence of complacency or euphoria. Birchenough, it must be remembered, is not only an educational historian of authority; he was also professionally engaged in educational work throughout the thirty-two years between 1905 and 1937: as school teacher, training college lecturer, and LEA inspector. (He was also an acute, not to say acid, critic of the errors and shortcomings of English education—and English educationists.)

The second illustration comes from a memorandum on the training of teachers prepared by a Joint Standing Committee of the Training College Association and the Council of Principals and published in 1939. 'The present time', says its Foreword,

is marked by great activity of thinking and experiment amongst those engaged in the training of teachers. *The growth of liberal ideas of education* has been reflected in the training centres . . . in most to a marked extent. In particular recognition of the need for continual experiment and development in educational practice and theory has long ago *demolished the idea that the business of Training Colleges was to provide a ready-made, stereotyped training in class management and method*.[7]

The third illustration is probably the most significant, for it shows profound change operating within a much shorter period of time than the others. Only twelve years separated publication of the Hadow Report on *The Education of the Adolescent* from that of the Spens Report on *Secondary Education with special reference to Grammar Schools and Technical High Schools*. Not only did the latter Report repudiate the judgment of the former about the claim of junior technical schools to be ranked as secondary schools; on an even more fundamental issue, the nature and purpose of a school, it shows that professional opinion had very considerably clarified during those years. Hadow declares that:

There appear to be two opposing schools of modern educational thought, with regard to the aims to be followed in the training of older pupils. One attaches primary importance to the individual pupils and their interests; the other emphasizes the claims of society as a whole . . .[8]

But Spens asserts, without a trace of doubt, that

a typical school of the present day is to be regarded as not merely a 'place of learning' but as a social unit or society . . . deliberately created and maintained as a means of bringing to bear upon the young formative influences deemed to be of high importance for their own development or for the continued wellbeing of the community.[9]

In all such pronouncements the dominant concern is the wellbeing of the child. As Mr Stanley said: 'We concentrate not so much on the subject as on the pupil . . . and on the pupils as human beings.' Birchenough noted the better opportunities given to teachers to study children by the Hadow reorganization of the elementary school; 'the enrichment of school life by new adjuncts to teaching' such as radio broadcasts and visual aids; and the emergence of a new concept of 'school' as 'a scene of varied social, intellectual, aesthetic, practical and physical activities; a place where the aim is to help each boy and girl to develop his potentialities not for any ulterior purpose but for his own sake'.[10]

Such changes do not emanate from a single source; a thousand influences, radiating from innumerable individual and corporate personalities, must coalesce, or clash, to produce them. 'To account fully for the broader views now incorporated in general educational practice', said the Spens Report, 'would involve a diagnosis of contemporary life, but it is clear that the newer ideas have entered into the main body of schools from several distinct sources.'

. . . some of the most significant have simply filtered down from the Public Schools . . . Others are an evident and direct response to the needs of an age which has seen an immense development in the political and industrial organization of all the great nations. Others, again, are expressions of a profound modification in the old individualistic basis of English life—changes in opinion and sentiment which require the schools to accept responsibilities formerly borne elsewhere. Lastly there has been a notable advance in the technique of education, accompanied and fostered by an incessant discussion of ends, ways and means, by no means confined to those whose interest in the subject is that of the teacher or the administrator.[11]

That passage may serve as a reminder—if such be needed—that change in education, be it forward, backward, or sideways (and all these forms occur, even today), does not, and cannot, come simply because theoreticians, or reformers, judge it desirable. It occurs, and must occur, within the context of society, and it must be acceptable to at least substantial elements in that society. And the last sentence in the passage is also a reminder of another irrefutable fact of life: that 'ends, ways and means' must be translated into terms of techniques before they can be effective in schools. Many a desirable reform still stands outside the schools, waiting for that translation to be made.

The closing years of the nineteenth century and the first three decades of the twentieth were, happily, exceptionally rich both in philosophers who rethought the ends and aims of education and in practitioners who attempted the difficult task of translating these into practice. The names of some are still world-renowned: John Dewey, A. N. Whitehead, Bertrand Russell—pre-eminently philosophers, but all three to some extent practitioners as well; Binet, Burt, Spearman, Thomson, Thorndike among the scientists; Badley and Neill among outstanding teachers. The names of others should not be allowed to pass completely into oblivion: for example, W. H. D. Rouse, who succeeded marvellously with a 'direct method' of teaching the classics; his colleague Caldwell Cook, whose 'Play Way' in English language and literature profoundly influences the work of many present-day teachers who have never heard of his name; Norman MacMunn, pioneer of creative self-government for children; A. J. Lynch, leading English protagonist of the American Helen Parkhurst's 'Dalton Plan'.

Lynch was for many years a member of the New Education Fellowship, founded by Beatrice Ensor, ex-HMI, and the Swiss Adolphe Ferrière in 1920. In the English section of the Fellowship were soon to be found a number of independent schools whose sole common characteristic was that they believed in 'freedom'—spiritual, intellectual, physical, moral—for both children and adults, teachers and taught. Great harm was done to children by a few self-centred extremists whose concept of freedom was patterned according to a rigid formula; but these apart, this small group of 'Freedom' schools, which included Bedales, Frensham Heights, St George's, Harpenden, and Summerhill, made an immensely valuable contribution to English education in the fields of human relations and informal teaching methods.

Milk in Schools scheme

Other manifestations of a new humanity in the world of school derived directly, as the Spens Report said, from the needs of the times. The mass unemployment of the 1920s and 1930s led to a renewed concern for children's health. Investigations made disclosed widespread undernourishment. In 1931 the Ministry of Agriculture launched a campaign to induce school children to drink more milk. This developed into the Milk in Schools scheme organized by the governmentally sponsored Milk Marketing Board. Under this scheme school children could buy, on every school day, one-third of a pint of milk for a halfpenny. Necessitous children, who in those days were all too numerous, were given the milk free; and those who showed signs of malnutrition —and they, too, alas, were numerous—were in many cases given twothirds of a pint. In the 'depressed' areas, that is, areas of more than usually heavy unemployment, LEAs and voluntary organizations provided a service of midday dinners, free or at a nominal charge, for necessitous children—a service which certainly saved the lives of some at least of the poor little half-starved wretches.

But the public concern for children's health was not restricted to underfed and undernourished children; it covered all school children. In 1930 the Board of Education issued a pamphlet on playing fields for schools—which were common enough as adjuncts to secondary schools, but up till then almost non-existent for elementary schools. Six years later the Board demonstrated that it really meant business about this; it requested those LEAs which had not provided playing fields for their schools to do so without delay. At the same time it urged all LEAs to appoint adequate staffs of physical training organizers—no unnecessary injunction, seeing that only about a third had any PT organizers at all.

In 1936 also the Board of Education issued a handbook of *Suggestions for the Planning of Buildings for Public Elementary Schools*; and despite the enormous publicity given to the Physical Fitness Movement launched in the following year (Women's League of Health and

A. J. Balfour

Sir Robert Laurie Morant

R. A. Butler

James Chuter Ede

Emily Davies

Anne J. Clough

W. E. Forster

T. H. Huxley

Lyon Playfair

Children being rounded up for the Board School, 1874

London Board School lavatory, 1885

Prize day at a Board School, 1875

Opposite

Dinner time at a Board School, 1889

A penny dinner for Board School children, 1885

Physical training, 1881

A drawing class in the early 1900s

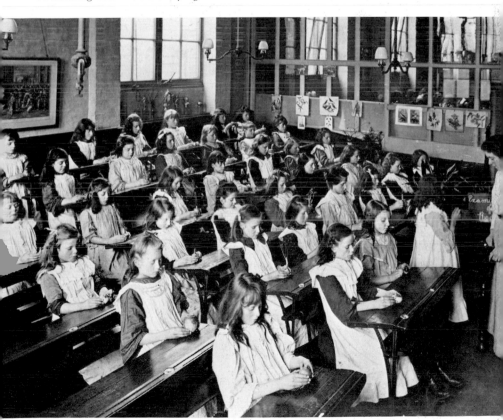

Nature study class in an Elementary School, 1908

cf. "Women in Love"

School milk, 1937

BBC broadcast to schools, 1945

Beauty, and all that), it is possible that this handbook was of more lasting benefit to the country's children than all the measures directly promoting physical fitness or training. Not because of any particular types of building advocated in the *Suggestions* (though they were on the whole extremely good), but because of the basic principles it laid down—principles which today are taken for granted, but which only thirty years or so ago were either quite novel or completely ignored in practice. Such as, for example, that the planning of school premises should be related to the type of school that would use them; that craft rooms were needed in primary as well as secondary schools; and that —believe it or not—attractive interior decoration was as appropriate for schools as for homes.

It should never be forgotten that all these official and voluntary initiatives, and the innumerable recorded and unrecorded experiments conducted in schools of all types during the later years of the 1930s were carried out against a background of mounting public anxiety. This reached its climax on the first of September 1939, when Hitler invaded Poland. Britain, instead of raising the school leaving age—due, of all ironics, on that very day!—began instead a mass evacuation of over a million children from supposedly dangerous areas to supposedly safe ones.

All normal educational activities ceased, all reforms were halted. The Education Act 1936—that poor little pennyworth of half-baked compromise—was put into cold storage. So was the Spens Report. Even a £12 million scheme for expanding technical education was shelved—a strange preamble to a technological war. It looked as though advance was at an end indefinitely.

But never was it more true that the darkest hour comes just before the dawn.

Notes

1. *The Education of the Adolescent*, HMSO, 1926, Introduction, p. xxi.
2. R. H. Tawney, ed. *Secondary Education for All*. A policy for Labour, published for the Labour Party by Allen & Unwin, 1922, p. 7 (*Tawney's italics*).
3. In the pamphlet *The New Prospect in Education* (1928), and through the Inspectorate.
4. See Chap. VII pp. 91–106 and pp. 150–206 in the original edition.
5. *Teachers and Youth Leaders*, p. 49.
6. *History of Elementary Education in England and Wales*, 3rd edn., University Tutorial Press, 1938, p. 450.

7. Pp. i and ii. The Memorandum, entitled *The Training of Teachers*, was published by the University of London Press. (*Italics mine.*)
8. *The Education of the Adolescent*, paragraph 102.
9. *Secondary Education with special reference to Grammar Schools and Technical High Schools*, chap. IV, para. 9.
10. Birchenough. *History of Elementary Education* . . ., p. 450.
11. Spens Report, chap. IV, para. 9.

Part Three

Infancy of a New Era

6

Wartime Planning

The Government's purpose in putting forward the reforms described in this Paper is to secure for children a happier childhood and a better start in life; to ensure a fuller measure of education and opportunity for young people and to provide means for all of developing the various talents with which they are endowed and so enriching the inheritance of the country whose citizens they are.

The British Government's White Paper on *Educational Reconstruction*, presented to Parliament in July 1943.

Those words were written in the middle of a major war, before victory was even in sight. The planning of the reforms they refer to had begun almost as soon as the war started. Within three months of its outbreak, in November 1939 the Government, mindful of the exploitation of young people during the first World War, called into being the Service of Youth, a partnership of statutory and voluntary bodies to provide physical and cultural facilities for young workers in their leisure hours. Before that partnership had got into full running order hints were coming from the Board of Education that it was contemplating reform on the grand scale. They received an almost embarrassingly widespread welcome: from teachers and educational administrators, from the political parties, the Churches, industry, the trade unions, parents, and members of the general public.

What touched off the almost universal clamour for reform which ensued—whether it was dirty evacuees or propaganda by pressure groups—really hardly matters at this date. What does matter is, first, that root and branch reforms—'no tinkering!'—were demanded with surprising unanimity by practically everyone professionally engaged in public education, and secondly that the reforms proposed summed up almost all the aspirations felt and the experiments tried by teachers and educational administrators over half a century. The near unanimity of professional opinion (and indeed of public opinion) became more and more evident as replies were published, from all sorts of organizations, to questions put to them by the Board of Education in a 'Green Book' which that Department distributed, as Professor W. O. Lester Smith has so aptly put it, 'in such a blaze of secrecy that it achieved an unusual degree of publicity'.[1] This document, issued early in 1941, gots its nickname from the colour of its cover. It was supposed to be highly confidential (no one ever explained convincingly why), but actually did no more than gather together all the proposals for the reform of the English educational system (other than the patently impracticable) which had been made over the previous two or three decades, and invite comment upon them.

Most of the organizations which were sent the Green Book replied volubly, and with no pretence at secrecy. Many sent their replies simultaneously to the Board of Education and the Press. From the ferment of discussion thus provoked there emerged two critical problems which necessitated long and delicate negotiations: the position of the voluntary schools and the future of the Part III authorities. Not until July 1943 was the President of the Board of Education, R. A. Butler, able to present to Parliament, and the public, in the White Paper *Educational Reconstruction*, the Government's proposals for post-war educational reform. These were, with one exception, very favourably received. The Part III authorities hotly contested their proposed replacement by 'district committees'—and got this altered.

The 1944 Act

Events thereafter marched swiftly. In December 1943 Mr Butler introduced into Parliament an Education Bill embodying the White Paper's proposals. On 3 August 1944, after debates of a harmony that would have staggered the combatants of 1870 and 1902, the Bill became law as the Education Act 1944.

The detailed provisions of this great Act should be studied in the original text. Among its numerous important reforms five were to my mind outstanding: first, the reshaping of the statutory system to enable it to offer to all, a continuously progressive education, arranged in three end-on stages, of primary, secondary, and further education; second, the statutory duty laid upon the LEAs to secure adequate facilities for all three stages; third, the extension of secondary education to all children, with its important corollary that, secondary education being compulsory for all, no tuition fees could be charged for it in schools maintained by the public authorities; fourth, the ingenious compromise whereby voluntary schools could select their status according to their willingness to pay for denominational rights; and last, but far from least in this short list, the provision forbidding the disqualification for appointment, or dismissal, of a woman teacher solely because she was married—a reform which has had a greater effect upon the composition of the teaching profession than any other made in the twentieth century. Many minor modifications have been made in the Education Act 1944 during the quarter of a century since it was passed; but none of these basic reforms has been touched.

Just two months before the Education Act was passed the Government published the McNair Report on the Supply, Recruitment and Training of Teachers and Youth Leaders. This Report, by a departmental committee of ten persons appointed by Mr Butler in 1942, is chiefly remembered today for the recommendations (made by only half the Committee) which resulted in the coordination of all teacher training in geographical regions, each (with one exception) under the direction of a university functioning through an area training organisation (ATO) representative of all the partners in the enterprise: university, training establishments, LEAs, teachers.

But other recommendations made by the McNair Committee (and by the whole Committee, not only part of it) were equally important, and should not be forgotten: first, that there should be recognized in primary and secondary schools only one grade of teacher, the 'qualified teacher'; second, that there should be one basic scale for all qualified teachers, with additions for special qualifications or experience, throughout the country; third, that the 'pledge', whereby students committed themselves to serve as teachers in maintained schools for a stated period of years in return for a subsidized university education, should be abolished; and fourth, that the ban on the employment of married women as teachers in maintained schools should be removed. Controversial though some of those recommendations were felt to be at the time they were all accepted by the Government, and have all stood firm.

University expansion

Throughout the years in which the Education Act 1944 was being prepared and passed, planning was going on equally vigorously, though with much less publicity, in the field of university education. There was, however, a very considerable difference in emphasis. In the changes proposed, and made, in the statutory system the emphasis was almost wholly on reform, on betterment. In the field of university

117

and other higher education, while the idea of reform was certainly not ignored, the main attention was given to problems of physical expansion, and means for financing this.

In 1941 the British Association for the Advancement of Science appointed a committee to study all aspects of the development of university education in the United Kingdom after the war. In 1943 this committee produced a series of reports. The one on finance said: 'The Treasury grant [to the universities and university colleges] should be at once doubled after the war.' (It had been stabilized throughout the war at the 1938–9 figure of £2,149,000.) The number of students, the committee thought, should be immediately increased to 50 per cent more than the 1938–9 figure, that is, to about 75,000. Both these estimates were modest by comparison with others made at the same time. The Parliamentary and Scientific Committee, an unofficial but influential non-party body comprising MPs and professional scientists, wanted the Treasury grant nearly trebled, to £6 million or £7 million, and looked forward to 'an ultimate doubling of the total numbers enjoying university education'. The National Union of Students, with the endearing optimism of youth, called for a three- or four-fold increase in the number of students within ten to twenty years—and wildly Utopian as this seemed to their elders at the time, they were the nearest right; in 1966, twenty years after the postwar expansion of the universities got going on a large scale, there were well over three and a half times as many full-time students in the universities of Great Britain as in 1938–9: 184,500 as against 50,000.

In June 1943 the Committee of Vice-Chancellors and Principals, which had become during the war the recognized spokesman for the universities, asked the University Grants Committee to 'set on foot a review of the financial implications of the expansion *which national policy would require the universities to undertake*, both in the immediate future and in the next ten or twenty years'.[2] The wording of that request was, considering who made it, of the utmost significance. The Committee of Vice-Chancellors and Principals had not the right (and never have had) to commit their universities or colleges to any decision or act of policy; but it is extremely unlikely that they would have inserted the clause linking university expansion to national policy without feeling pretty sure that they could carry most if not all of their academic and administrative colleagues with them. For that clause implied a completely new relationship between the British Government and the British universities. To accept that the universities would expand at the dictates of 'national policy'—and, of course, be paid out of public funds for doing so—did not necessarily mean any infringement of academic freedom, of the right to teach and to learn at the dictates of one's intellectual conscience; or, as it is so often put, 'to pursue the truth wherever this might lead'. But it most certainly meant a large encroachment upon the independence of universities as corporate bodies.

The University Grants Committee replied to the Vice-Chancellors' request by inviting the universities and university colleges to draw up development plans for the following ten years, including estimates of the capital and maintenance costs involved. That was in November 1943. The plans were with the UGC early in 1944—which strongly suggests that they had been ready in draft for quite some time. The UGC, after prolonged discussions with the universities and colleges, forwarded to the Treasury an agreed statement about costs, and a memorandum emphasising that 'the expansion and improvement of facilities for university education which the public interest demanded could be achieved only with the aid of largely increased subventions from the Exchequer'.[3]

Early in 1945 the Treasury agreed, and in April the Chancellor of the Exchequer announced (i) that the annual grant to the universities and university colleges during the first two years after the war would be £4,149,000—two million pounds a year more than previously; and (ii) that the grant would be substantially increased during subsequent years. The promise was kept; the annual grant was by 1947–8 double the 1945–6 figure, and by 1951–2 had risen to £16,600,000.

Among the recipients from 1945 onwards of Treasury grants were the University Colleges of Hull and Leicester, previously small and struggling private institutions; the result was an astronomical increase in the numbers of their full-time students—something like tenfold in five years.

During the war years and those immediately following a veritable battery of governmental and other committees investigated postwar needs in many fields of professional education. Some reported before the war had ended; in 1944, for example, reports were presented on Medical Schools (the Goodenough Report), Veterinary Education, and Teachers and Youth Leaders (the McNair Report); all demanded a considerably larger intake of students for their particular speciality, as did practically all the sectional committees which reported during the following few years.

Two reports of more general significance were those presented by the Percy and the Barlow Committees. The Percy Committee on Higher Technological Education (Chairman, Lord Eustace Percy, President of the Board of Education from 1924 to 1929), was appointed by R. A. Butler in April 1944 'to consider the needs of higher techno-logical education in England and Wales and the respective contribu-tion to be made thereto by Universities and Technical Colleges'. The Committee's answer to the delicate question of 'respective contribu-tions' was fourfold:

1. Industry must look mainly to universities for the training of scientists, both for research and development, and of teachers of science;
2. [industry] must look mainly to technical colleges for technical assistants and craftsmen;
3. both universities and technical colleges must share the responsi-bility for educating the future senior administrators and technically qualified managers of industry;
4. neither university nor technical college courses are designed of themselves alone to produce a trained engineer.

To remedy the deficiency stated in (4) the Committee proposed the institution of a course for engineers equal in length to a university first degree course, but made up of alternate periods of full-time study and works practice—today's widely used 'sandwich' course. This recom-mendation was to lead ultimately to some of the most spectacular changes made in British higher education since 1945, including the creation of a number of 'technological' universities. Unhappily, these changes were preceded by years of sterile controversy about—of all things—whether the award for such an engineers' course as the Percy Committee proposed should be a degree or a diploma. It was not until 1956–7 that even the sandwich courses really got going. A most regret-table and wasteful episode, whose only value was that it illustrated, all too sadly, how the feuds of vested interests (in this case the univer-sity and the technical college) can obstruct and delay advances known by all to be desirable, even urgent.

Scientific manpower

No such controversy attached itself to the conclusions and recommen-dations of the Barlow Committee (Chairman, Sir Alan Barlow, a joint second secretary at the Treasury). This committee was appointed by the Lord President of the Privy Council in December 1945 with the following very wide remit:

To consider the policies which should govern the use and develop-ment of our [i.e. Britain's] scientific manpower and resources during the next ten years and to submit a report on very broad lines at an early date so as to facilitate forward planning in those fields which are dependent upon the use of scientific manpower.

Rarely can any committee charged with so great a responsibility have worked so swiftly. The Barlow Report,[4] which was largely to determine the character and size of the postwar expansion of higher education in Great Britain for at least a decade was presented to the Lord President in April 1946—barely four months after the Committee was appointed. (It was published in May.)

The crucial conclusion reached by the Committee was that 'the immediate aim should be to double the present output [of professionally qualified scientists], giving us roughly 5000 newly qualified scientists per annum at the earliest possible moment'.[5] The Barlow Committee agreed with the Percy Committee that it was the business of the universities to produce these scientists.

It is only to the Universities that we can look for any substantial recruitment to the ranks of qualified scientists. The proportion that has come from other sources in the past is very small indeed and we do not favour any attempt to add a responsibility for producing a substantial number of pure scientists to the existing and prospective burdens of the Technical Colleges [which] will be hard put to it to produce the number of technologists that are required to support and apply the work of the scientists.[6]

The Committee had no doubt that the universities could do the job —even though it had asserted that the doubling of the number of scientists should be paralleled by comparable increases in the numbers of students of other subjects. But it agreed with the Committee of Vice-Chancellors and Principals that the Government must provide the money: 'The great bulk of the money required for university development must come from the Exchequer . . . more than any other single factor, the universities' response to any call for expansion will depend upon a wise and generous financial policy towards them on the part of the Government'.[7]

Thus by the middle of 1946 the stage had been set for action at the levels of both school and higher education. The main lines of policy had been determined; what now confronted the nation was the frighteningly difficult task of implementing a policy which implied advance along the entire educational front during a period of acute shortages in the three essentials for any material advance: manpower, money, and goods of all kinds. Inevitably, some parts of the policy fell by the way, while others had to be substantially modified. But there were notable successes, and it is with these that the next chapter will mainly deal.

Notes

1. W. O. Lester Smith. *To Whom do Schools Belong?* 2nd edn., Blackwell, 1945, p. 202.
2. *University Development from 1935 to 1947.* Report of the University Grants Committee. HMSO, 1948, p. 76 (*italics mine*).
3. *Ibid.*
4. *Scientific Man-power: Report of a Committee appointed by the Lord President of the Council,* Command 6824. HMSO, 1946.
5. Report, p. 8.
6. Report, p. 6.
7. Report, pp. 11–12.

7

A Sea of Troubles

Freedom, variety, elasticity are, and have been, the merits which go far to redeem the defects in English education, and they must at all hazards be preserved. The 'system' which we desire to see introduced may rather be described as coherence, an organic relation between different authorities and different kinds of schools which will enable each to work with due regard to the work to be done by the others, and will therewith avoid waste both of effort and of money.

From the Report of the Royal Commission on Secondary Education (the Bryce Report), 1895, vol. i, p. 326.

If ever English education had a chance to start afresh, it was in 1945. A National Government had passed through Parliament, with the unanimous approval of all the political parties, an Education Act which promised reforms of the first magnitude. Public opinion was as solidly behind the Act as was Parliament. Everyone wanted action, and speedily; the only crime was delay.

The 1944 Act did not, it is true, extend to university education. But in this field two crucial policy decisions had by 1945 been made which could hardly fail to bring massive changes in their train. The first, which was discussed at length in the previous chapter, was the decision to expand very substantially the number of university students, and to pay for this expansion out of public funds. The second was the decision, first announced in April 1943, to mount a Governmental scheme of 'further education and training' for the benefit of men and women who because of war service—either military or civilian—had had to interrupt or defer their post-school education or training for a career. This scheme, which covered all the countries in the United Kingdom, and was jointly administered by the Ministries of Agriculture, Education, and Labour, and the Scottish Education Department, was designed to secure an adequate supply after the war of men and women able to occupy posts of responsibility in industry and the professions. It dealt largely, therefore, in awards tenable at universities and other institutions of higher education. The numbers involved were very large; by the end of 1949, when the scheme was drawing to a close, over 83,000 awards had been made by the English Ministry of Education. Of these, nearly 44,000 were held at universities. All the awards were for full-time courses.

Before looking at other successful educational enterprises carried through during, roughly, the first half-dozen years after the war, it is perhaps advisable to recapitulate some of the formidable obstacles which had to be overcome in order to ensure the success of any educational enterprise undertaken during these years. The obstacles were of two kinds: mental and material. The latter, naturally, attracted the public attention, but the former were, in my opinion, just as daunting. Possibly even more so.

'In nothing, not even in religion, has the innate conservatism of the human race been more marked than in education', wrote A. F. Leach[1] over half a century ago. In 1945 few people in England and Wales *wanted* to be 'conservative'; almost all were in favour of advance in every field of social welfare: in education, health, housing, insurance . . . the lot. What slowed down progress in all these fields was the almost universal fear, usually not overtly expressed but always there, of *revolutionary* change, of going too far, or too fast, or both. This led inevitably to a tendency to hedge, to compromise, to doubt the wisdom of this, that or the other radical proposal, to delay, even to oppose.

Two curious instances of this 'innate' conservatism (hitherto, so far as I know, unremarked) are to be found respectively in the Education Act, 1944, and the 1945 agreement between the Treasury and the UGC. The preamble to the Education Act describes it as 'An Act to reform the law relating to education', that is, to *reshape* it—not to *replace* it with something entirely different. Even Mr Butler, its chief and principal architect, claimed only that his Act *recast* the existing educational system. Which is precisely true; the 1944 Act is a reshaping of the 1902 Act. Similarly, the Treasury–UGC agreement stipulated that the proposed university expansion should be *aided* by *'largely increased'* subventions from the Exchequer; that is to say, the existing *mode* of financing university education was to be retained, the difference (and certainly this was striking) being in the relative sizes of the shares contributed from statutory and voluntary sources. Incidentally, the UGC was at the time so antipathetic to the idea of unconventional change that it set its face firmly against the foundation of *any* new universities.

A second very serious cause of psychological impediment to advance was the lack, or failure, of communication, and so of coordination, between the bodies entrusted with carrying out policy decisions. The passing of the Education Act 1944, and the Treasury–UGC agreement of 1945, for example, were decisions of national policy of the first importance. Yet signs of coordination in their working out were so lacking as almost to suggest that these decisions were taken independently, by different sets of people, each completely unaware of the others' existence. (Whereas, in fact, each must have been a Cabinet decision.) So, unfortunately, it is not altogether true to say, as more than one educational historian has said, that the 1944 Act gave England and Wales a 'fully coordinated system of national education'. That will not, and cannot, be the case until the universities are an integral part of the system. (This may come to pass sooner than most people expect. It is just possible that the process of integration may have started in April 1964 when the English Ministry of Education was merged in the composite Department of Education and Science, headed by a Secretary of State with responsibilities towards all the universities of Great Britain as well as to the statutory system of education in England and Wales.)

The uncoordinated development of primary and secondary, further and university education, and of different categories of schools and colleges has always tended to make the pattern of English education complicated and overlapping. The fact that such uncoordinated development continued after 1945 until, at earliest, 1956, when the White Paper *Technical Education* began the process of rationalization, makes very difficult any attempt at a neat analysis of *advance* in education (as distinguished from mere growth of numbers and/or facilities) during the years immediately following the 1939–45 war. The greatest single obstacle to distinguishing between growth and advance (which are, of course, far from being synonymous) is the enormous amount of improvisation, of emergency action, that was forced upon those responsible for deciding and carrying out national and local policy during those years. Within the field of formal education (and excluding crises affecting all social welfare services), it is possible to specify six separate causes of such improvisation that were major handicaps to educational advance during the half-dozen years between 1945 and 1951.

First, the destruction and damage caused by enemy action to schools and colleges—conservatively estimated as affecting to a greater or lesser degree about one-fifth of all educational establishments. (The fact that it was a good thing that some of these premises were destroyed is highly gratifying, but irrelevant to the present argument; they had to be replaced.) Second, the serious dilapidation of others, due to requisitioning, or simply to inability to carry out normal maintenance during the war years. Third, the physical impossibility, because of the shortage of manpower, materials, and sometimes (though not always) of money, of putting in hand simultaneously all the reforms legislated for in the 1944 Act. This early caused the shelving of most reforms whose province lay outside the years of compulsory full-time education; notably, the provision of nursery schools and county colleges. Fourth, the unpredicted—and to be fair, unpredictable—rise in the birthrate. Fifth, an equally unpredictable passion for staying on at school beyond 'compulsory school age'. And sixth, a continuously expanding demand for post-school education of all kinds and at all levels, but especially for university education. This demand has persistently outrun all forecasts.

The effect of these various obstacles to straightforward reform persisted long after the immediate postwar years. It is hardly an exaggeration to say that throughout the quarter-century between 1945 and 1970 the overwhelming proportion of the manpower, money, thought and effort that have been lavished—that word is used deliberately—on public education in England and Wales has had to be devoted to two purposes, neither of which necessarily connotes advance: (i) providing 'roofs over heads' and (ii) recruiting and training sufficient teachers to keep the educational machinery ticking over. That during this process of ensuring enough quantity much attention has been given to quality is not only a tribute to those who have insisted on high standards; it has resulted in a number of notable educational triumphs.

One further word of warning. Since national policy for educational advance has so often during the past quarter of a century had to be diverted to meet particular needs or emergencies, there are still all sorts of unfinished jobs and loose ends. This makes it very difficult to feel sure which among the innumerable measures taken since 1944 with the aim of improving English education will in the long run prove beneficial. All that is claimed for those measures described in the rest of this chapter is that they seem to have done something to clear the way for advance.

Emergency training

One must begin, of course, with the supply of teachers, the most important consideration in any educational system. And start with the

Emergency Training Scheme. This was in operation for six years, from 1945 to 1951. It brought into the primary and secondary schools, from HM Forces and the war industries, some 30,000 men and women who had qualified as teachers by undergoing one year of intensive training. These emergency-trained teachers were expected to hold their own, as equals in every respect, with colleagues who had obtained their qualification in the normal way, that is, by two years of training. In my opinion, they have done so. (There have been, naturally, the inevitable exceptions.) They have done so partly because of their personal qualities, and partly because the Emergency Training Scheme (of which I saw a great deal) was one of the most imaginatively conceived enterprises ever undertaken in English education, and—despite the criticisms to which it was subjected—one of the most efficiently conducted.

Had it not been for the success of the Emergency Training Scheme the school leaving age could not have been raised in 1947–8—or if it had been the result might well have been a shambles. Raising the age in 1947 was a political act of faith—or, if you prefer less idealistic language—a political gamble. It came off, largely, though not, of course, exclusively, because of the sterling qualities of so many of the men and women the Emergency Scheme was sending into the schools. When I speak of the 'success' of the scheme I must be understood to mean, not the number of teachers it brought into the schools, indispensable though this quantitative reinforcement was, but the fine quality of many of the men and women it recruited. Their enthusiasm, their vigour, their stability, and their mature experience have continued to give confidence as well as learning to one generation after another of school children. And, an important but not often noticed consequence of the success of the Emergency Scheme, it undoubtedly encouraged the central and local authorities to seek to secure more 'mature' entrants into teaching.

HORSA huts

Logically, this account should now proceed to discuss the normal modes of training teachers. But before coming to this epic story, may I remind readers of two other emergency schemes, often forgotten today except perhaps as objects of mild obloquy? The raising of the school age would not—to put it mildly—have been so uneventful had there not been what I have elsewhere described[2] as 'an emergency building scheme which, though less spectacular, was in its way as great a triumph as the Emergency Training Scheme for Teachers'.

I refer to HORSA (Hutting Operation for the Raising of the School Age). Like the Emergency Scheme for Teachers, HORSA had serious teething troubles. The huts, provided by the Ministry of Works, were at first indignantly refused by many LEAs. They were criticized by the Royal Institute of British Architects[3] as 'inconvenient in use, substandard in accommodation, uneconomical to heat, erected on playing space, and unnecessarily costly'. They were accepted, reluctantly, only when it became brutally clear that otherwise secondary schools would be grossly overcrowded—however many church halls the LEAs might hire. There followed a race against time. It was not quite completely successful; but by the summer of 1948, when all the fourteen-year-olds were in the schools, sufficient of the 5000 HORSA classrooms had been erected, and equipped with close on half a million SFORSA (School Furniture Operation for the Raising of the School Age) chairs, tables, desks, stoves and what have you, to have saved the day. For this the main thanks must go to the now defunct Ministry of Works and the men it employed; their effort was sustained, unremitting, and efficient.

'Saved the day.' Does this imply the assumption that raising the age from fourteen to fifteen—with no question of exemptions—was 'a good thing', a real point of departure for educational advance? In my opinion, quite certainly yes. It was, I believe, not merely desirable, but absolutely necessary, an inescapable national obligation. Even ten years of full-time schooling is all too short a period in which to acquire a sound foundation of rudimentary general education. That young people themselves realize this is shown by the steadily increasing proportion which either stays on at school beyond the age of compulsion or enters a full-time course in a college of further education. The raising of the school age to sixteen, which was due to coincide with the centenary of State education, but, regrettably has been postponed, will when it comes be equally acceptable to most fifteen-year-olds.

Expansion of training colleges

The ever increasing number of young people remaining in full-time education beyond the compulsory period has been, and still is, one of the factors complicating the supply of teachers. There are others yet more formidable. When the full story of the post-1945 expansion of the training colleges comes to be told, it will be found to be as rich a mixture of comedy, tragedy, and heroic saga as could be desired. Comedy, in the Shakespearian sense, in that most colleges, having survived a 'sea of troubles', have emerged, or are emerging, bruised, battered, and to some extent bewildered, but larger, stronger, more capable and more confident institutions. Tragedy, in that an unknown but certainly not inconsiderable number of college principals and senior academic and administrative staff were for years metaphorically buried under bricks and mortar. Some actually suffered serious impairment of their health, and many were unable, because of their preoccupation with buildings and rapidly rising numbers of students, to give to the educational aspects of training and the normal management of educational institutions the care and attention these demanded and deserved. Heroic saga, in that, amazingly, staffs and students almost everywhere managed, despite the bulldozers and pneumatic drills, not merely to maintain but to raise academic and professional standards. This despite also the tensions caused by erratic shifts in government policy, which did nothing to alleviate the physical discomforts of working amidst din, dust, and continual disturbance.

The story of this expansion, and reorganization, of the training of teachers is, in 1970, by no means at an end; and in fact one cannot yet see when, or what, the end will be. To give the story in any detail would require a volume of some size. All that is attempted here is to suggest that between 1945 and 1968 there appear to have been four broad phases, and to comment briefly on these.

Phase I   1945–46. Clearing the way for expansion.
Phase II   1947–51. Coordination of the training system.
Phase III 1952–57. Slow down and hesitation.
Phase IV   1958–68. Full steam ahead.

Phase I. In 1945 and 1946 the Ministry of Education announced financial arrangements which cleared the way—at least as regards money—for rapid expansion.[4] To the voluntary colleges, in 1945 numbering fifty-one out of a total of seventy-six recognized two-year colleges, the Ministry offered capital grants to cover up to one-half of the cost of any major additions or improvements to premises, and 100 per cent recurrent grants in respect of approved tuition and boarding fees, less parental contributions, assessed on stated income scales, towards the cost of boarding. For LEA colleges both capital and recurrent expenditure were henceforth to be paid from a national 'pool' to which every LEA had to make annual contributions calculated on the number of pupils in its primary and secondary schools. An immediate result of this sharing of costs was the opening of large numbers of new LEA colleges—there were nineteen within the first two years. Thus began the most significant shift of the centre of gravity in teacher training ever known in England and Wales. Until 1946 the voluntary college was the typical college; thereafter it has been the LEA college. In 1945 there were two voluntary colleges to every one LEA college. By 1968 the position had been reversed; there were two LEA colleges to every one voluntary college.

Phase II. During the years covered by this phase, roughly 1947 to 1951, the Emergency Training Scheme was running down, while the number of students in permanent training colleges was increasing rapidly; by 1951 it was well over twice as large as in 1938–9: 19,289 as against 8734. But the most important development in this phase was the setting up throughout England and Wales of Area Training Organizations (ATOs). In these were grouped, on a geographical basis, all the recognized training establishments for teachers. Of the seventeen ATOs created between 1947 and 1951 all except three—Cambridge, Liverpool, Reading—were headed by universities or university colleges. To serve as ATO headquarters and education centre an institute or school of education was established in each area; except in the three non-university areas it was created, housed, and staffed by the university or university college responsible for the area. (Liverpool and Reading later became university institutes.)

The terms 'ATO' and 'Institute of Education' have always tended to be regarded as interchangeable, but strictly speaking the ATO is a partnership representative of all the bodies in the area which are concerned with the training of teachers: the university, the LEAs, the colleges of education (as the training colleges have been called since 1965), the teachers, HM Inspectorate, and the Department of Education and Science. The institute (or school) consists of a building, and a salaried staff which carries out the instructions of the ATO. The nearest parallel is the local education *authority* (i.e. the county or county borough council) and its education *department*.

It is impossible to give any exact idea of the influence that the ATOs, and the institutes and schools of education have had on the teaching profession as a whole. The strongest impact has, naturally, been upon the colleges of education, and particularly on their staffs, who have been brought into much closer contact with colleagues from other colleges and the parent university. There is no doubt that college schemes of work and subject syllabuses, while they may not have been more carefully prepared (for colleges were always scrupulous about the preparation of both), have been greatly improved by being subjected to much more extensive scrutiny. (In institutes in which I have worked every scheme or syllabus was scrutinized by at least five different bodies, including the senate of the university, before being approved.)

But the ATOs have also been of considerable benefit to the teaching profession in other ways. All institutes and schools of education run advanced and refresher courses for serving teachers. All provide good specialist libraries. All encourage, and most engage actively in, educational research. Through their directors, almost all of whom, being professors, are members of senate, they exercise influence upon university and national policy for the education and training of teachers.

Phase III. This phase, extending over some five years (1952–7), was one of doubt and hesitation; of anxiety first about the supply, and then about a possible oversupply, of trained teachers; and finally of agonised appraisal and reappraisal of the pros and cons of lengthening the general course of training for non-graduates from two to three years—a reform which, incidentally, had been thought desirable by HMI sixty years previously, and had been the official policy of the training college associations for at least forty. In the end, the right decision was taken—and who will grumble because it was taken for the wrong reasons?

Three-year training

It is a curious story. In 1949 the Minister of Education set up a National Advisory Council on the Training and Supply of Teachers (NACTST). It was a very large body (many people thought too large), because it was representative of every conceivable interest concerned with the training of teachers. Nevertheless, it was for some years an extremely active body. Very early on it began to consider whether, and if so when, it would be practicable to do what the McNair Committee had strongly—not to say peremptorily—demanded: lengthen the two-year course to three years.

> A two-year course is not sufficient [said McNair] for students entering upon their training at 18 years of age. The studies and activities required of them and the claims of school practice are such that their day is overcrowded with things that must be done, leaving them little time for necessary recreation and reflection. . . . Many students in training colleges do not mature by living: they survive by hurrying.[5]

Unfortunately, the NACTST felt compelled in 1952 to advise that because of the very large number of teachers that would be required in the coming years to cope with larger numbers of children in school due to the increasing birthrate, an immediate extension of the training course seemed impracticable; in fact, the Council doubted whether the reform would be possible before 1960. This attitude was understandable, for at the time there was (justifiably) widespread anxiety lest the future supply of teachers should prove too small. In 1951 there had been empty places in women's colleges; and there were again in 1952. Not many, but sufficient to make people apprehensive. The training colleges, it was pointed out, were already getting nearly two-thirds of all grammar school girls who stayed at school until seventeen and did not go on to university. They could hardly expect to get a much higher proportion than that. And it was probably too much to hope that many more 'mature students' would come forward; surely the Emergency Scheme had drained that source of supply, at any rate for the time being?

Happily, in 1954 the supply situation improved, thanks, said the Ministry of Education,[6] to 'buoyant recruitment, later retirement and the continued willingness of married women to remain in or return to teaching'. Similarly encouraging net increases in the teaching force were shown in 1955 and 1956. The Ministry of Education, with what seems incredible naïvety, began to look forward to a time when 'the school population begins to fall'.[7] The Association of Teachers in Colleges and Departments of Education (ATCDE) (formed in 1943 by the amalgamation of the Training Colleges Association and Council of Principals) naturally began to press again for the introduction of a three-year course. In 1955 the Minister of Education, Sir David (later Lord) Eccles, asked the NACTST to consider this matter once more. In 1956 the NACTST advised that the early 1960s seemed to 'offer a peculiarly favourable, possibly unique, opportunity' for lengthening the course, since—and here, in the Council's own words, is the astonishing reason:

There is a limit to the number of additional teachers which the schools can absorb and the country afford in a period of declining school population. Without introduction of the three-year course or some other equivalent restriction of recruitment (and without some major new source of demand for teachers), it is not impossible that there may be some difficulty in the early 1960s in maintaining full employment in the teaching profession.[8]

And that was how the three-year course came about: as 'a measure to adjust the rate of recruitment to the needs of the schools in the 1960s', by reducing 'by about one-third the output from the present two-year colleges'.[9]

And then, almost as soon as Sir David Eccles had fixed 1960 as the date for starting the three-year course, there came the awful moment of truth. The Ministry's projections of the annual increase in the teaching force were wrong! The NACTST had been led to reckon on net annual increases in the teaching force of 7000 up to 1960 and (with two-year training) 6000 thereafter. But in 1957 there was a net increase of 4400 only. Women were leaving teaching in quite unexpectedly large numbers. And after a slight lull, the birthrate was rising again. And, more pupils than ever before were staying at school beyond fifteen.

To the Government's credit, they stood by their promise to lengthen the training course. To be able to fulfil it, they ordered that an immediate increase in the number of training college places be put in hand. And so the story moves into *Phase IV*, the phase of 'full steam ahead'. From 1958 to 1968 there was an accelerating increase in the number of students in training to be teachers. In 1958 it was under 30,000, in 1968 over 90,000.

Such a spectacular increase should have solved the problem of staffing the schools. But the sad fact is that it did little more than preserve the existing teacher-pupil ratios, because of the colossal 'wastage' among women teachers. The trends towards earlier marriage and child-bearing meant in England and Wales that of every ten young women trained to be teachers, six would have left the profession within five years and eight within ten years. This huge wastage was to some extent counterbalanced by an increasing recruitment of 'married women returners'—qualified women teachers whose domestic commitments had become less exacting—and of 'mature students'—unqualified men and women of any age between twenty and fifty-plus who are prepared to undergo two or three years' training. By 1966 these two categories made up 18 per cent of all students in training to be teachers. As persons, and as teachers, very many of these people are most acceptable; but in the nature of things many, especially among the women, are 'immobile', that is, can only teach within easy travelling distance of their homes; and most of them do not live in the areas in greatest need of teachers, the socially depressed areas. Many, too, because of domestic commitments can only teach part-time, which makes them particularly vulnerable in times of national economic stringency—such as that which began in 1968. The cut-back, in some LEA areas in the use of part-timers and 'returners', which persisted in 1969, may indeed herald the onset of a Phase V, in which the emphasis will be on productivity, not numbers.

The effects of the wastage among women teachers are felt most severely in the infants schools, since these are staffed exclusively (with the rarest exceptions) by women. Nevertheless, the postwar infants school has maintained, and indeed enhanced, its long-established reputation of being both an extremely happy place and a very progressive institution. So has the junior school, despite the fact that it had for twenty years (and still has to some extent) to cope with the pressures of the 'eleven-plus', the so-called 'examination' (actually, a battery of intelligence and attainment tests) used to determine who should go to the coveted grammar school.

'Eleven-plus'

The tragedy of the 'eleven-plus' is, in my opinion, the most deplorable that has darkened English education since Lowe's Revised Code of 1862. I cannot imagine why we did not foresee what would happen. Every attempt we have made in this country to select by examination for places carrying superior status—be it in school, university, civil service, industry or the professions—has quickly became a bloodstained battlefield of cutthroat competition. Why did we all (a few honourable exceptions apart) allow ourselves to be bemused into believing the (doubtless sincerely meant) aspiration of the 1943 White Paper that 'in the future, children at the age of about eleven should be classified, not on the results of a competitive test, but on an assessment of their individual aptitudes, largely by such means as school records'?[10] It sounded so good; and so we forgot the lessons of history —including that of the immediate predecessor of the eleven-plus, the 'special place' examination—'the scholarship' as the general public ignorantly, but quite correctly called it. We forgot, too, that it has always been impossible either to restrain the ambitions of socially ambitious parents for their young or to defeat their manoeuvres. Because we forgot all this, an inordinate amount of anxiety, exasperation, pain and suffering was endured during the 1950s and 1960s by innumerable parents, and by some (though by no means all) of their children.

But let us be perfectly clear *what* caused this anxiety and suffering. Not the examination, but its alleged (and often actual) consequences. 'No English school is ever really happy,' the late Sir Fred Clarke used to say, 'unless it has another it can look down upon'. The appalling misfortune of the secondary modern school was that for years after its promotion in 1945 from elementary to secondary status not only did every other type of school look down upon it, but also large sections of the public—and I fear many teachers as well, including not a few who were serving in secondary modern schools. Despite all the obloquy to which it was subjected, despite the dreadful feeling of rejection, of inferiority, that many children were alleged to have experienced because they 'failed' to secure a place in the grammar school, despite even the horror stories (some of them at least partially true) about bad secondary modern schools, I still adhere to the belief I formed in the late 1950s, that on the whole the secondary modern school has been one of the greatest triumphs in post-1944 English education, and of inestimable benefit to many hundreds of thousands of girls and boys. And may I add that during the years 1945–68 I visited more secondary modern schools, in more parts of the country, than all except a very few people.

Some of my reasons for that belief I gave in a short book published in 1958 which I called an 'interim report' on *Secondary Modern Schools*. It was based on the visits I had made up till then, including two round-the-country surveys made specifically to discover what the schools were doing—and feeling. Today, a dozen years later, I am compelled to revise some of those reasons, because during these years the secondary modern school (or a large part of it) dramatically changed direction.

Every student of the recent history of the English educational system will remember the ecstatic promise made in 1945 by Miss Ellen Wilkinson, the Minister of Education,[11] that the new 'secondary modern' schools should be 'free from the pressures of any external examination', in order that they might 'work out the best and liveliest forms of secondary education suited to their pupils'. And much extraordinarily good and extremely lively *secondary* education was, in fact, worked out in numerous schools all over the country. I saw examples of it as far apart as North Yorkshire and South Dorset, East Suffolk and West Wales.

General Certificate of Education

But many schools were baffled by this new freedom; they yearned for a yardstick, for some externally determined measuring rod by which they might assess the success, or otherwise, of what they were doing. So, when in 1947 the SSEC recommended to the Minister of Education that the examinations for the School and Higher School Certificates should be replaced by a single examination (which could be taken at two levels) for a General Certificate of Education, secondary modern teachers here and there pricked up their ears. What riveted their attention was the fact that this proposed General Certificate would be obtainable on fundamentally different terms from those for the School Certificate and Higher School Certificate. There were three crucial differences:

1. The examination for the School Certificate was a *grouped* examination. The examinable subjects were arranged in four groups; and candidates had to select, according to specified conditions, a minimum of five subjects, of which at least one had to come from each of the first three groups (Group 4, arts and crafts, did not count towards a pass), *and they had to pass in five subjects to secure a Certificate.* (Most candidates took six or seven—to allow for accidents!)

   The examination for the GCE was to be a *subject* examination. There were no groups, and no conditions about what subjects must be taken. A pass in a single subject would secure a Certificate.

2. For the School Certificate whole classes of pupils had to be entered. For the General Certificate individual entries were to be accepted.

3. The School and Higher School Certificates were granted on the results of two separate examinations, of which the second (for the Higher School Certificate) was ordinarily taken two years after the first. In theory, one could bypass the School Certificate and take only the Higher School Certificate, but as the School Certificate, passed in appropriate subjects at a sufficiently high level, exempted the holder from the entrance examinations of British universities (and professional associations) it was most unwise to do so.

   The Ordinary and Advanced levels of the GCE, being separate parts of the same examination, carried no such restrictions. Papers at either, or both, levels could be taken at a single sitting.

The reactions of the different types of secondary school to the new examinations, first held in 1951, were most illuminating. The grammar schools, although they had been advised by the SSEC to defer taking the examinations until towards the end of a pupil's school career, and with able pupils to bypass the Ordinary level, set out to make the new examination scheme as like the old as possible. In this they were aided and abetted by the universities, with whom they agreed in 1949 that exemption from the latter's entrance examinations could only be secured by what was in fact a grouped certificate, as below:

1. A pass in English Language and in either four or five other subjects.

2. These subjects had to include (i) a language other than English, and (ii) either mathematics or an approved science.
3. At least two subjects had to be passed at Advanced level.

The grammar schools also persistently memorialized the Ministers of Education to lower the permitted minimum age for sitting the GCE examination, which had been fixed at sixteen. In 1952 they succeeded in extracting from Miss (later Dame) Florence Horsbrugh a typically English compromise. Sixteen would remain the minimum age for entry, but heads of schools could enter younger pupils if they were prepared to certify (i) that it was educationally desirable for such pupils to take the examination in given subjects at the proposed time; and (ii) that such pupils had worked so well that they would probably pass. And that was that. No more trouble about the minimum age. The grammar schools entered their pupils *en masse* for Ordinary level at sixteen, or earlier, so as to get the supporting subjects out of the way and allow a clear two years, or longer, for university aspirants to make sure of getting two, or more, *good* Advanced levels. A very wise precaution; competition for university places was already hotting up.

The grammar schools' reaction to the GCE was predictable. So, I suppose, were those of the secondary modern schools. There were three quite different sets of reactions. Some schools with indifferent or low academic standards, and those schools which had not yet outgrown the old elementary school concept of post-primary education—well, it is hardly an exaggeration to say that they couldn't have cared less. GCE? That was a grammar school affair. It was no concern of theirs. Secondly, teachers who had welcomed rapturously Ellen Wilkinson's assurance that the secondary modern schools should be free from external examinations, and who believed with all their hearts that it was 'essential' to 'retain this invaluable freedom', refused, on principle, to have anything to do with the GCE, or, for that matter, with any external examination. Thirdly, there were the schools—and I must emphasize that amongst them were many of the best, the most progressive, of the secondary modern schools—which, as I mentioned earlier, had for years been looking for a 'yardstick' (how often I heard that word used!) by which to measure what they felt to be the increasingly impressive attainments, especially the academic attainments, of their intellectually more able pupils. In the GCE 'O' level examination they saw at once the yardstick for which they had been longing. It seemed almost tailormade for them. Gone was the hurdle of having to secure five passes at a single sitting—which they had realized was probably too high for most of their pupils. Gone was the obligation to enter for certain subjects, and—perhaps the greatest relief of all—gone was the necessity to enter the whole class, including the duds on the back row. A certificate for a single pass, in any subject one liked . . . what more, or rather, what less, could be desired? They began entering candidates. Some schools struck in boldly, entering a dozen or more candidates, and confidently predicting a score or more the following year. Other schools began more cautiously, entering only one, two, or three candidates, and making no promises about following years. By 1953, however, some three to four hundred schools were entering just over 4000 candidates. Ten years later, more than 1000 schools (over a quarter of the total number of secondary modern schools) were entering over 60,000 candidates.

It would be of little value to elaborate here the controversy as to whether external examinations are 'a good thing' for secondary modern schools. There is no consensus of opinion among secondary modern school teachers. Some whom I respect greatly have always told me most emphatically: 'No.' Others, whose judgment I respect equally, say just as emphatically: 'Yes.' The latter claim that when their pupils realize that they can do academic work at a far higher level than they (or their parents) ever imagined they get a spectacular boost to their morale, and that this results in higher standards of behaviour and of discipline as well as of work. They claim also that this improvement tends to spread throughout the school. The anti-examination Heads say all these good effects can be secured without putting pupils into the straitjacket of examinations; that external examinations restrict syllabuses, discourage experiment, initiative, and discovery, kill the whole idea of education as initiation into the realm of scholarship and skill.

The truth is that both are right according to their own lights. Some teachers can best bring out and nurture children's ability and aptitudes through the purposefulness and stimulus of some external spur, such as the idea of success in an examination. Others do it by different means, and by the use of different incentives. This is the English way. 'The only uniformity of practice . . . that each teacher shall think for himself, and work out for himself such methods of teaching as may be best suited to the particular needs and conditions of the school.'[12] Long may that remain the case in English education.

What made the secondary modern school, for all its indifferent units, one of the most successful enterprises of twentieth-century English education is, first and foremost, that it was served by teachers who had faith enough in their pupils to believe that they had ability hidden away in them, and who had sufficient enthusiasm, energy, sympathy, and professional expertise to bring it out. Not least successful were those who, in terms of normal 'results', had little to show, and who had nothing to do with GCE or any other external examinations; the dedicated volunteers who took on the 'backward' and 'remedial' classes. Their triumphs, all too little publicized, were paralleled by the superb work of so many of their opposite numbers in special schools for children handicapped by 'disability of mind or body'. 'Special educational treatment', be it in ordinary school, special school, hospital, or the child's own home, was improved out of all recognition during the quarter of a century between 1944 and 1969. That bold assertion cannot, unfortunately, be documented here, for it would take far too much space; but the evidence is to be found by those willing to search for it in reports of the Department of Education and Science, of the Chief Medical Officer, and of LEAs, and in unofficial comments by authors and contributors to the educational and general Press.

School building

First, foremost, and all the time, in any educational system, it is the teachers who matter most. But it is the gravest error to say (as is often said): 'Teachers matter, but *not* the buildings.' In fact, the buildings matter a very great deal. Good buildings, well equipped, make both teachers' and pupils' work easier as well as more agreeable. And, fortunately, a very great number of very good buildings has been erected in England and Wales since 1944. (There are also some horrors, and too many that are shoddily finished.)

It is perhaps going too far to say that the present generation of school architects is the first to have realized fully the educational importance of beautiful premises, but it does seem to be the first which has successfully combined beauty with function. (At any rate, in interiors; many exteriors are dull, and some ugly. Architects claim that this is due to lack of money.) For this increasingly happy marriage between appearance and function much credit must go to (i) the lively Architects and Buildings Branch created in the Ministry of Education in 1949, (ii) the LEAs who have been courageous enough to cooperate with the Branch in designing and erecting experimental buildings (which could so easily have proved expensive misfits), (iii) the many architects in private practice who have cooperated in, and helped to bring success to, these adventurous enterprises, and (iv) the various educational building consortia, the first of which was CLASP (Consortium of Local Authorities Special Programme), established in 1957, which have so notably improved school building techniques and materials.

I think that, without forgetting its less happy examples, one can agree that English school building over the past quarter of a century has added up to a superb performance, unequalled for all-round excellence in any age or country. Many countries (chiefly among the so-called 'underdeveloped' countries) built more schools during this same period, and here and there you will find more beautiful or more elaborately functional buildings; but nowhere, so far as I know, quality combined with quantity on such a generous scale. It is, too, a fair tribute to those who have been, and are, engaged on this enterprise, to say that rarely have they rested on their laurels; their triumphs have served to inspire them to seek for even better ideas. Because of this continuing search for the combination of beauty with function, the next few decades may well see an absolute revolution in school building. Up to 1968 evolution rather than revolution had been the dominant urge; only one or two of the most advanced projects really broke away from the conventional 'so many children, so many rooms' concept.

For there to be an absolute revolution in school building there must be a comparable revolution in the organization of school communities. There are two aspects of this, which I may perhaps label loosely the 'overall' and the 'cellular'. The first concerns the make-up of the entire body of pupils assembled in a 'school', the second the distribution of those pupils on (or off) the site. Until quite recently school organization has been in both respects of a blinding simplicity. One took a straightforward age range—primary (5 to 11+), or secondary (12 to 15+), for example—and fitted so many children in that age-range into a single building (or set of buildings), which was divided into a given number of cells, called classrooms, according to the anticipated number of children attending the school. All the pupils in a school arrived at the same time, stayed there for the same number of hours, had the same breaks, and with few variants did lessons of the same length in the same kind of cell; and the life of the entire school was regulated by the same code of discipline. All this was (and is) in flat contradiction of even the most rudimentary principles of children's physical, mental, and emotional development; and so as frustrating as could well be of children's abilities and aptitudes—which the 1944 Act specifically says parents, teachers, and educational administrators must encourage and nurture.

Happily, the early 1960s saw the beginnings of several breaches in this traditional belief in universal rigidity in school organization:

'vertical classification', or 'family grouping', in primary schools; the freedom in the choice of age limits for schools introduced by the Education Act of 1964; various types of 'open-plan' primary school buildings, ranging from tiny ones like those in some Oxfordshire villages to the large Eveline Lowe school in south-east London; Newsom-type workshop-cum-club annexes for non-academic fifteen-year-olds, and library-cum-lounge-cum-cafeteria annexes for sophisticated sixth-formers.

Such developments, actual and projected, were by 1970 no more than straws in the wind, uncertain indicators of the direction change may take. In any attempt to estimate the significance for the future of what happens in the present it is essential to try to distinguish evolutionary changes, which generally take place for purely educational reasons, from consciously planned changes, which are often the result of rationalized political motives. A most interesting example of evolutionary change during the quarter-century under discussion was the gradual transformation of a number of secondary modern schools into comprehensive schools—in fact though not always in name. In their early days they built up a wide range of 'practical' subjects and 'biased' courses. With the coming of the GCE they introduced academic streams, and thus became in effect 'bilateral' schools, with 'grammar' and 'modern' sides. As their biased courses—especially the GCE course—grew in popularity more and more pupils stayed on beyond 'compulsory school age', and the schools developed, first, a fifth year, and later in many cases a sixth form. Without having consciously aimed at it, many of these schools reached a point at which they were providing all the forms of secondary education needed by normal English children.

A somewhat comparable instance of evolutionary growth is to be found in the development of the grammar school sixth form during the same period. It is, unfortunately, not nearly so happy a story. Formerly —that is to say between the First and Second World Wars—the sixth form in a maintained secondary school was a tiny intellectual élite, made up for the most part of gifted children expected to win open scholarships at Oxford or Cambridge. They lived, like the gods of classical antiquity, on Olympian heights, remote from ordinary mortals, and served only by highly selected staff. (A teacher who was allowed to take the Sixth had indeed arrived.) With the opening of the universities after 1945 to all who could secure two or more 'A' levels, the numbers in sixth forms rocketed, until in many schools the sixth form has become merely the unwieldy top half of the school. The supply of scholarly teachers competent to deal with sixth form work was always limited, and is today much too small to cope with the vast and increasing numbers. Yet competition for university places grows keener, and so, alas! in too many cases the mob gets fed with processed food, predigested to produce 'A' levels. And not even the Schools Council has yet found the answer.

Among the consciously planned changes affecting primary and secondary education much the least publicized, but certainly not the least important was the elimination of the 'all-age' school. This was a really remarkable achievement, and it was carried through with far less bitterness and recrimination than might have been feared, seeing that most of the 'all-age' schools were Church schools. In January 1947 there were in England and Wales 8755 'all-age' schools, containing over one million pupils; in January 1967 there were 72, containing just over 20,000 pupils. Within twenty years, that is to say, over eight and a half thousand schools—more than a quarter of all the maintained schools in the country—had either been closed or had had their function restricted—with almost no public fuss.

It is possible, and to some people very natural, nostalgically to regret 'the passing of the little village school'. (In cold truth, while many of the 'all-age' schools were small village schools, many were neither in villages, nor small. They were down-town slum schools, often housing hundreds of pupils. And many of those in villages have not 'passed', but have become primary schools.) The simple fact is that unless the country were both able and willing to spend astronomical sums on staff, laboratories, gymnasia and so on for handfuls of children of secondary school age, genuinely secondary education is today not possible in small schools, and still less so in departments of small schools.

Comprehensive schools

Far and away the best known, and the most controversial, planned change in English secondary education begun during this period was the change from the single-purpose to the comprehensive school. To document fully the tortuous history of this transition would require a book in itself. Here are offered only some half-dozen brief notes upon it.

First, the organization of secondary education on comprehensive lines is far from being unique to England and Wales, who are actually among the latecomers in this field. Comprehensive secondary education has long been practised in Australia, New Zealand, Scotland, the USA, and the USSR, and has in recent years been spreading in

Europe, especially in Sweden, where by 1968 it was widely established. But, secondly, the reasons for adopting it, and the forms adopted, have been different in each country. The reasons have ranged from sheer necessity—too sparse a population to sustain a school unless every child in the district attended it—to a high degree of political sophistication. It is probably true to say that in most countries a political impulse has been strong, not to say dominant: the desire to guarantee social justice to all the young by ensuring that all shall have equal opportunity in education—especially those under-privileged socially or economically. This has meant that in some countries it has been assumed, without adequate evidence, that social and educational benefit must automatically ensue from a comprehensive organization of secondary education. This was notably the case for years in England and Wales, where both this assumption and the contrary one—that no benefit could possibly ensue from comprehensivization—were widely and confidently made long before there were any comprehensive schools in the country.

(It cannot be too strongly emphasized that in educational issues only evidence from within one's native culture is completely reliable. I learned this in 1950, when I made an extensive tour in the United States to see American comprehensive schools, and the following year, when I saw comprehensive schools in Austrialia and New Zealand.)

Such shadow boxing (one cannot concede it a more dignified name) went on in England for at least twenty years, from the publication of the Spens Report in 1938, which really set it going on a large scale, until, at earliest, 1958, when the first genuinely comprehensive schools in the country were old enough to begin to offer a few straws of tentative evidence. But even in 1970, twelve years later, with comprehensive secondary education made the national policy, and with over one-sixth of the nation's secondary schools organized on comprehensive lines, there is still, in the opinion of reputable researchers, insufficient evidence to justify or refute the claim that comprehensive schools are better *educational* instruments than other types of secondary schools. Even less evidence has yet been published to support, or deny, the sociological claim that if children drawn from all ranks of society and representing all levels of ability and all varieties of aptitude and interests are educated together in a single set of school buildings they will, for that reason, inevitably learn to live together in a spirit of mutual tolerance and understanding. Even if this were proved to be so, there remains the organizational problem of ensuring that the pupils in any given school do in fact add up to a representative cross-section as defined above. In a densely populated and class-conscious country such as England, where people tend to reside in class-differentiated districts, this can be extremely difficult. London has for some years been trying to cope with this problem by allocating quotas for each school of measured intelligence levels, and transporting children from outside a school's catchment area to make up any deficiencies. Since the children brought in from outside have to be selected, this policy could conceivably make a comprehensive school as highly selective as many a grammar school.

Quite another policy might derive from the terms of Mr Anthony Crosland's famous Circular 10/65.[13] The *educational* significance of that Circular was almost wholly overlooked, attention being concentrated on the *political* aspect. But the Government's sanction of other forms of comprehensive school than the 'all-through' school taking children from eleven to eighteen could have extremely important consequences. It could give a completely new look to the concept of comprehensive secondary education. It would certainly make this concept much more complex. First, by the mere fact of replacing the idea of one kind of comprehensive school by the idea of several kinds; and secondly, and more importantly, by introducing a whole range of quite new organizational, curricular, and methodological problems. The purely educational problems of the 'all-through' comprehensive school are essentially the same as those of any large school, and so are more or less familiar. But two-tier, and even more three-tier, schemes pose genuinely novel problems of size, siting, premises, age ranges of pupils, curricula, examinations, discipline, and—far from least important—the relative attractiveness to staff of each type of school. Apart from the limited Leicestershire experiment with a two-tier organization which began in 1957 there was as late as 1969 virtually no evidence on which to rely about such matters.

Experiment and research

But structural reorganization of the English educational system is only part, and possibly the least important part, of the profound change which is taking place in English education today. One can foresee the possibility, in the near future, of a revolution in school building, and in the organization of school communities—of which the organization of secondary education on comprehensive lines is an early, and not very revolutionary, step. But in respect of what is to be taught in schools, and how this may best be taught we are in 1970 well over the threshold of a revolution comparable in scale with that which took place during the first three decades of the twentieth century.

And, may I suggest, comparable with it in other aspects as well! To a revolutionary of those ancient days it is ironically gratifying to find ideas being acclaimed in the 1960s as 'new' with which we experimented in the 1920s. But it is good that they are again the subject of experiment; and for three reasons they stand a far better chance of being successfully developed in the 1970s than they did fifty years previously. First, the experiments of the 1920s were most of them conducted in single schools, if not in single classrooms, and (in maintained schools at any rate) usually by teachers who had no idea that there might be similar experiments being conducted at the same time in other schools or classrooms. Moreover, not only did these teachers work unsupported by the encouragement of others of like mind; all too frequently they had to contend with contempt, hostility, or obstruction from colleagues. Secondly, very little organized research was being undertaken in Britain, and still less published, upon problems of school organization, discipline, curriculum and method. (The Scottish Council for Research in Education was not formed until 1928, the National Foundation for Educational Research in England and Wales not until 1945, and the Schools Council, that indefatigable instigator of curricular research, as recently as 1964). Thirdly, there were in the 1920s only very unsophisticated visual and auditory aids available to teachers. In making that general statement I am not forgetting the BBC's school broadcasts, begun in 1924, and from the start excellent. But reception was often poor, and anyhow most schools had no receiving sets and were not likely to have any unless they bought or made them themselves. I was refused one by a relatively enlightened LEA; and it took the school two years to build it with components purchased for the physics laboratory.

Today elaborately controlled educational researches and experiments are conducted on a national scale, with very large subsidies from both public authorities and philanthropic organizations. It may be premature to suggest that the day of the 'lone wolf' experimenter in school or class is over, but the signs suggest that it is drawing to its close. The teacher with the urge and the capacity for experiment and/or research, will tend to become one of a team working under the aegis of the Schools Council, the National Foundation for Educational Research, a university institute or school of education, or some other body professionally equipped to undertake research and experiment on a large scale. Finance, the nightmare of the single experimenter, will no longer trouble him, nor be his concern. Funds will be forthcoming from his sponsoring body, which will have got them in bulk from the Department of Education and Science (by 1968 distributing over £1 million a year on research) or one of the great independent foundations. The danger that collective organization of educational research could lead to a uniformity of curricula and methods which is repugnant to British minds is obvious, but can surely be avoided; and nationwide, controlled, experiment based on the validated results of research should bring about a general improvement in the content and methods of teaching and learning. I for one would be prepared to risk the danger for the sake of the benefit, being among those who believe that there is rather too much difference between the standards and techniques of individual English schools.

Nationally organized and financed research and experiment may also supersede the time-honoured method of seeking to discover the road ahead by means of Royal Commissions, *ad hoc* committees, standing Advisory Councils, and the like, which work by collecting opinions (courteously called 'evidence') from interested bodies, and attempting to arrive at a generally acceptable compromise between the welter of conflicting views. The Robbins and the Plowden Committees, which spent respectively £67,000 and £45,000 on scientifically mounted surveys and other researches to substantiate their findings may be prototypes of the machinery for investigation in the future.

Some such machinery, geared to operate continuously, will be an absolute necessity in the future, because of the ever-increasing size, range, complexity and importance of the educational system in any society where the rate of political, social, economic and industrial change is rapid or accelerating. During the first third of the 'century of growth' which is the subject of this book, the term 'public education' meant in England 'elementary education' (and that meant not much more than the '3 Rs') for working-class children between the ages of five and thirteen. During the second third the term was expanded to include secondary education for a few as well as elementary education for the many. The final third is taking in the entire range of 'further' education, including university education, which has been made at long last available to anyone with the ability and the energy to undertake it.

Notes
1. In *Educational Charters and Documents 598 to 1909*, Cambridge University Press, 1911, Introduction, p. ix.
2. In *Growth in English Education 1946–1952*, Routledge & Kegan Paul, 1954, p. 19.
3. In a memorandum issued early in 1946; quoted from *Growth in English Education*, p. 23.

4. See Circular 85, *Revised Regulations for the Training of Teachers*, 12 February 1946.
5. Report, p. 65.
6. *Education in 1955*, p. 10.
7. *Education in 1956*, p. 43.
8. *Three Year Training for Teachers*, 5th Report of the NACTST, HMSO, 1956, p. 7.
9. *Ibid.*
10. *Educational Reconstruction*, p. 9.
11. *The Nation's Schools*, Ministry of Education Pamphlet No. 1, p. 21.
12. *Handbook of Suggestions for Teachers* . . ., 1905.
13. *The Organization of Secondary Education*, 12 July 1965. In this the Secretary of State 'requested' LEAs to submit plans for reorganizing secondary education on comprehensive lines.

8

Explosion

Throughout our Report we have assumed as an axiom that courses of higher education should be available for all those who are qualified by ability and attainment to pursue them and who wish to do so.

The Robbins Report on *Higher Education.*[1]

It is as certain as anything can be which lies in the realm of conjecture that the problems of higher education will dominate the minds of all concerned with the provision of public education in England and Wales throughout the remainder of the twentieth century. This is not, of course, to suggest that the problems of primary and secondary education have been solved, or that they will demand less serious attention in the future than they have received in the past. It remains every whit as true as it was in the far-off days of the early mechanics institutes that no satisfactory higher education is possible unless it is based on a sound foundation of primary and secondary education. And upon the content, and the mode of acquisition, of that fundamental education will depend the quality and the character of any subsequent higher education. The curricular and pedagogic reforms in primary and secondary education which were in hand, or projected, in 1970 will be of immense importance not only in their own spheres but also as determinants of the higher education to which ever larger proportions of the nation's children should proceed—in fact, *must* proceed if England is to stand up to the challenge of the Atomic Age.

But when everything possible has been done to render preparation for higher education both excellent and appropriate, there still remains the actual process of higher education. It is clearly axiomatic that this should be as excellent, and appropriate, as the earlier education. Which means, on the material level, that the facilities provided must be fully adequate, that is, must measure up to individual and societal needs—anticipated as well as actual—and must be efficiently used by both learners and teachers. To what extent, and in what ways, has the post-1944 expansion of facilities for higher education in England and Wales measured up to these exacting requirements? To judge by much contemporary criticism, hardly at all. But the English are notorious self-denigrators; they can hardly bear to think they have done anything well. 'Not bad' is almost the upper limit of self-praise they will allow themselves. Sometimes this is all that is due; at other times it is a vast understatement. In England's large and varied expansion of higher education over the past quarter of a century there have been deficiencies, defects, and weaknesses. But there have been also great triumphs. As a first example, consider the huge growth in the number of *full-time* students in non-university institutions: from 42,000 in 1947 to 197,000 in 1967—or 220,000 if sandwich course students be included. A fourfold increase in twenty years. Numbers alone, of course, may mean nothing more than . . . numbers; but the importance of that particular growth lies in the fact that it indicated a change of heart. Before the 1939–45 war the English did not really believe in full-time higher education; not outside universities, at any rate. They did not even believe in part-time education during the daytime, that is, during 'working' hours. Only the hero who piled Pelion on Ossa by swotting in night school after sweating all day in employment really commanded their approbation.

The trend towards full-time courses, and the shift of vocational studies from the evening to the daytime are among the clearest indications that the pattern of higher education in England and Wales has been drastically altered since 1944. It is still being altered; what the final pattern will be (if ever there is a final pattern) is in 1970 anyone's guess.

Within the narrow limits of a single chapter it is impossible to examine more than a small sample of the changes that took place or were initiated in English higher education between 1945 and 1970. All I have attempted has been to select a few of those which seem to me of major significance, and to offer some personal comments on them. If these comments are often critical, this implies no derogation of the courage and energy that have gone into making the changes. Nor, certainly, should my comments be considered as *ex cathedra* pronouncements, but only as fallible opinions whose value should be rated by the amount and quality of discussion they provoke. Discussion of what we are doing in education is essential, more essential than ever before; we are experimenting on an unprecedentedly large scale and in more, and more varied, ways than ever we have done previously. We must, so far as we can, make sure we are doing the right things in the right ways.

Doubtful policies?

I begin—of course—with the supply and training of teachers. In two respects this was, between 1958 and 1968 at any rate, the most successful of all the enterprises in English higher education; the proportionate increase in the number of students, and of the facilities provided for their training, exceeded that in any other field. This despite the fact that the return in trained manpower (or, to be more accurate, woman power) was proportionately far less. The 'brain drain' of British scientists across the Atlantic was numerically infinitesimal by comparison with that of women teachers into marriage and motherhood. Yet as late as 1969 no national policy seems to have been envisaged other than pouring in more and more fully trained recruits to repair the huge losses: a policy as wasteful as it is expensive.

This is one facet of policy in English higher education about which I have always had the gravest misgivings. A second is the almost universal disposition, not least in official circles, to regard university education as the only reputable (even genuine) form of higher education. This disposition has been manifest in the overwhelming priority given by successive governments to university expansion, in the absolute distinction drawn—up to 1969, at any rate—between the administration of 'autonomous' (i.e. university) institutions and 'non-autonomous' (all the rest), in the relative status of the academic staffs, and in the resentment felt by young people when they 'fail' to get into a university, and are compelled, if they wish to continue their education, to make do with some secondrate establishment such as a technical or teacher-training college.

The expansion of university education since 1945 has been a prodigious achievement. Directly the 1939–45 war was over the number of full-time students began to escalate. By the autumn of 1945 it had exceeded the prewar peak. By 1947 it was over 50 per cent larger. By 1960 it was twice as large, by 1965 three times, by 1969 over four times. Vast sums were poured into buildings. New universities were created. Yet so large has been the demand for places that every year thousands of qualified applicants have been denied admission. But what about other forms of higher education? Teacher training establishments—a very special case—have been expanded even more rapidly; other further education establishments far less so. In the year 1968–9 there were about 180,000 full-time students in the universities of England and Wales; in all types of 'non-autonomous' colleges other than training colleges for teachers there were fewer than 100,000 students, full- and part-time, doing courses of higher education comparable in standard with university courses.

If university education is but one among several distinguishable types of higher education, these figures suggest a serious imbalance. It cannot surely be that the most academic type of higher education is the appropriate one for nearly twice as many students as for all the other types, especially in so practically-minded a nation as the English? Yet authoritative attempts have been made to justify such a proportion. The Robbins Committee demanded that by 1980 there should be 350,000 students in British universities, and 145,000 in teacher training colleges, but asked only for about 65,000 'full-time advanced students in further education'. These proposals were implicitly defended in the following passage:

> It is sometimes said that, if other institutions became more attractive to students because of the wider availability of degrees, the pressure for entry to universities as a group will be eased . . . it would be wrong to allow considerations such as these to affect our judgment of *what is ultimately desirable and right.*

> The over-riding consideration that, in our view, outweighs [all] other arguments is the undoubted gain to young people of being brought into contact with leaders of thought and of knowing themselves to be members of an institution in which the highest standards of intellectual excellence are honoured . . . the atmosphere of the university can transform the whole approach to learning of students who, when admitted, seemed only doubtfully fitted for university work . . . *A large university population within the total provision for higher education is therefore something we conceive to be in the nation's interest, if the talents and abilities of our young people are to be called out.*[2]

That passage contains enough tendentious material to keep any intelligent seminar debating for a week. But the Robbins Committee was not uttering any new or original thoughts; this attitude had been implicit in the actions of every Government since the war, and had apparently been accepted unquestioningly by public opinion. While the Robbins Report was being prepared it became explicit in the intense municipal competition to acquire one of the proposed new universities. A direct consequence of the Report was the creation of a degree-granting body for the outcasts not in universities; an indirect one the governmental foundation of an 'Open University' for students not in any institutions at all.

The Keele experiment

For some years after the 1939–45 war the University Grants Committee—against the advice of the Barlow Committee—discouraged the idea of creating any new universities; postwar expansion, it thought, could and should be carried by the existing institutions. This did not prevent its putting the hitherto privately maintained University Colleges of Hull and Leicester on its grant list, and of encouraging a round of promotions from university college to full university status which lasted for ten years and added five new universities to the English total: Nottingham (1948), Southampton (1952), Hull (1954), Exeter (1955), and Leicester (1957).

These were the last of their kind. Only one new university college has been created since 1945, and that on utterly different terms from any previously. Early in 1946 Dr A. D. Lindsay, Master of Balliol, the Reverend Thomas Horwood, Vicar of Etruria, a district in the Potteries, and other members of an advisory committee which had been set up to investigate the chances of a university in Staffordshire, put before the chairman of the UGC, Sir Walter Moberly, a scheme for a completely novel type of institution. In this students would concentrate on one of two main subjects: (i) the social sciences and (ii) physical chemistry, but would also read 'supporting' subjects. The UGC rejected the proposal on both financial and academic grounds, but suggested amendments which might make it acceptable. In 1947 the Staffordshire Committee came back with a revised scheme, which was accepted by the UGC. The essential points in this scheme were (i) a four-year undergraduate course, (ii) the first year of this to be a 'foundation' year, in which all undergraduates would pursue a common general course, designed to give an understanding of the heritage of Western civilization, of the nature of modern society, and of the nature, methods and influence of the experimental sciences, (iii) in the subsequent three years undergraduates would read four subjects, two of them at 'principal' level, the other two at 'subsidiary'. Principal subjects would be studied throughout the three years, subsidiary for one year only, (iv) of the four subjects, one at least had to be chosen from the humanities and social sciences, and at least one from the experimental sciences.

Such a plan of studies could not be fitted into the framework of the London external degree. It was therefore agreed that the proposed University College of North Staffordshire should be entitled to grant its own first degree, of Bachelor of Arts with Honours, if it could secure the sponsorship of three established universities. Oxford,

Birmingham, and Manchester were induced by Lindsay to undertake the task. In 1949 the College was established by Royal Charter. In October 1950 Dr A. D. Lindsay, as the first Principal, welcomed the first students.

The story of how 'Sandy' Lindsay became Keele's first Principal is so moving that it must be included here. Lindsay had been searching for a suitable man, and thought he had found him. But another university offered this man a post, which he accepted. For the College planning committee this was an extremely serious setback, for the Privy Council had approved the foundation of a University College of North Staffordshire provided two conditions were fulfilled: (i) that three universities would act as its sponsors (that had been met), and (ii) that a suitable Principal was found. At this point the Reverend Thomas Horwood, as chairman of the committee, took the law into his own hands. He went secretly to Oxford, asked Lindsay if he had another candidate in view, and when Lindsay replied: 'No', said bluntly:

'Master, you come to us instead. It was you we always really wanted . . .' Lindsay . . . looked out of the window, on to the street below, for a few moments. Then he said rather coldly, 'Well you know, Alderman, what the doctors say, that I have about three years to live'. 'Then come to us for those three years!' cried Horwood.[3]

Unfortunately, the doctors were very nearly right; Lindsay outlived their estimate by eighteen months only. He died on 18 March 1951. But he lived long enought to launch successfully the most revolutionary experiment in university education that England had ever known—though not long enough, alas, to nurture it through to maturity. Had he been spared, he would no doubt have been acutely frustrated by the College's slow physical growth; though it opened with 150 students (which meant, automatically, 600 in its fourth year), it had only 850 when, twelve years later, it became in 1962 the University of Keele. For this slow rate of expansion there were three reasons: (i) the greater cost of a four-year undergraduate course; (ii) the fact that from the start the college was completely residential, for staff as well as students, thus involving much additional building; and (iii) a disposition in official circles to go slow until the success of the experiment had become apparent.

No such leisurely progress was allowed in the next round of university foundations. When during the middle 1950s the pressure on university places increased, instead of, as had been expected, lessening when the flood of ex-service applicants dried up, the UGC began to look favourably on the idea of founding some new universities—the idea it had so firmly rejected less than ten years previously. But it acted with circumspection. When in 1955 the Brighton Borough Council resurrected its proposal for a University College of Sussex (which the UGC had turned down in 1947) the Committee prefaced its consideration of this by taking a long cool look at four important general questions:[4]

1. How many new institutions were likely to be needed?
2. What sort of institutions would be required to meet future needs?
3. Where should such new institutions be located?
4. What procedures should be followed to ensure sound foundations?

Criteria for new universities

As the result of its deliberations, the UGC reached four crucially important decisions:

1. Any new institutions should be given from the start the power to grant at least first degrees. The principal reason for this was (in the Committee's opinion) that new institutions might be better able than old to 'experiment in the organization of university teaching and the design of university curricula'.
2. 'Any new institution should aim at not less than 3000 full-time students as a minimum target.'
3. As all the buildings of a university should if possible be on the same site, a minimum site of 200 acres would be required.
4. During their early years at any rate, new institutions should concentrate upon arts, social studies, and pure science. Existing institutions seemed capable of producing all the doctors, dentists, agriculturalists, foresters, and veterinary scientists that would be needed in the foreseeable future. Technology, similarly, seemed well provided for in the existing universities and the Colleges of Advanced Technology.

In February 1958 the Chancellor of the Exchequer announced for the four years 1960–3 a provisional university building programme of £60 million. This amount was to include the cost of making an early start upon buildings for a University College of Sussex. Towns all over Britain pricked up their ears, and within the following three years formal enquiries had reached the UGC from twenty-eight localities (twenty in England, eight in Scotland), most of which (along with others) later submitted proposals for new universities. Ultimately, the UGC selected eight (seven in England and one, Stirling, in Scotland). Of the seven in England, all but one, Colchester, had made application in the 1940s.

Sussex opened in October 1961. It was followed in 1963 by East Anglia (at Norwich) and York, in 1964 by Essex (at Colchester) and Lancaster, and in 1965 by Kent (at Canterbury), and Warwick (at Coventry). All were from the start full universities.

All these universities are based on relatively small towns (four of them cathedral cities), and all are located, not actually in but just outside their towns. This was deliberately planned. In 1959, after taking widespread advice, the UGC reached the following conclusions about the location of new universities: [5]

1. The reason why the 'Redbrick' universities were in the centre of large cities or conurbations was that originally most of their students attended part-time, and lived at home.
2. As university education became full-time the need to locate universities in large conurbations diminished, especially as plans for expanding the colleges of advanced technology ('in essence, embryo universities', the UGC called them) were in an advanced stage.
3. On the other hand, a university 'should be part of the community in which it lives'; the new universities must therefore not be 'put in the "green fields"'.
4. 'A supply of suitable lodgings, at reasonable prices' was desirable, since the new universities could hardly expect to be at first largely residential.
4. Most important; the area must be attractive to academic staff.

Point 2 has not gone uncriticized.

The growth of these seven universities has so far been astronomically rapid. Sussex started with fifty students; within five years it had 3000. The others began with larger initial enrolments—two, three or four, even five hundred—but nevertheless several doubled their student population annually for the first few years. Warwick, for example, opened with 400 students (300 undergraduates and 100 graduates); two years later it had 1500. This university intended from the start to be quite large within a relatively short time, and ultimately very large by British standards; both it and Essex have talked in terms of 20,000 full-time students. Such numbers are small by comparison with those in the universities of many other countries, but, London excepted, unprecedentedly large for Great Britain. What is even more important than their rapid physical growth is that each of these seven universities incorporates experimental features; in academic organization, in the content and arrangement of courses, in the design and use of teaching and living accommodation. The most striking departure in academic organization is the substitution in some of the universities—Sussex and East Anglia were the first—of 'schools' of related subjects—European studies, Biological sciences, for example —in place of the conventional Faculty made up of independent subject departments. As a member of a school an undergraduate will 'major' in one subject but must also study others cognate to it. Thus in European studies a student selecting a language would support it by studying, say, the history, literature and political institutions of the country or region concerned. Original architectural design is well illustrated at York: a complex of colleges that provide both teaching and residential accommodation—the latter for at least half of the students at any given time.

From diploma to degree

Hardly had the last of these universities opened their doors before another batch began to arrive: the transmuted Colleges of Advanced Technology (CATs). Theirs is a very strange story, with, one hopes, a very happy ending. In 1956, following ten years of strife between universities and technical colleges, chiefly about whether the latter should be allowed to award degrees, the Government decided to rationalize the organization of technical education in non-university institutions on a hierarchical plan. A pyramidal structure was to be erected on a base of some 300 'local', or 'district' colleges. On this base would be superimposed strata of 'area' colleges (say 150), 'regional' colleges (perhaps 25), and a very small number (probably not more than 10) of Colleges of Advanced Technology. Local and area colleges would undertake, respectively, elementary and intermediate studies. The regional colleges and the 'CATs' would do only advanced studies, that is, studies adjudged to be of degree or post-graduate level. In 1957 the long dispute about awards was settled, or so it seemed, by the creation of a high-ranking non-university award, called a *Diploma* in Technology (Dip. Tech.). It was not a *degree*, but it was officially rated as academically the equivalent of a first degree with honours of a British university. The refusal of the title of degree was a bitter defeat for the technical colleges, but some at least of their leaders realized that the Dip. Tech. offered a unique opportunity to demonstrate that other forms of scholarship besides the academic scholarship of the university had sufficient intrinsic merit to justify an award as distinguished as a degree but deliberately given a different name. The CATs and the regional colleges tried very hard to make the best use of this opportunity. They achieved considerable success. Year by year the number of students taking Dip. Tech. courses mounted, and of Diplomas awarded. Industry on the whole liked the Diplomates, feeling they 'belonged', since recurrent periods of training in employment were a required element in every Dip. Tech. course. A reputable alternative to the continuous full-time university course was, it seemed, being established. Then, just as the Dip. Tech. was becoming a really worthwhile qualification, it was abolished. The Robbins Report, published in October 1963, recommended[6] that the CATs 'should in general be designated as technological universities', with (of course) 'power to award both first and higher degrees'. And 'with the assumption of degree-granting powers by the Colleges of Advanced Technology, the National Council for Technological Awards will cease to deal with them'.[7] In other words, no more Dip. Techs. The Government accepted both recommendations. In 1966 and 1967 eight of the ten CATs received Royal Charters making them full universities. They were:

Aston in Birmingham, formerly Birmingham CAT;
Bath, formerly Bristol College of Science and Technology;
Bradford, formerly Bradford Institute of Technology;
Brunel, formerly Brunel College of Technology;
City, formerly Northampton CAT, London;
Loughborough, formerly Loughborough College of Technology;
Salford, formerly the Royal CAT, Salford;
Surrey, formerly Battersea College of Technology.

The Chelsea College of Science and Technology became a School of London University, and the Welsh College of Advanced Technology a constituent college of the University of Wales.

Non-university degrees

All these institutions began to transfer their Dip. Tech. students to degree courses before they had received their university charters. Meanwhile another, completely unprecedented, development was taking place in English higher education; students in non-university establishments were getting their own degree-granting body.

Staggeringly novel though this seemed, it was in fact a perfectly logical consequence of the second basic principle which had been assumed as axiomatic by the Robbins Committee: 'the principle of equal academic awards for equal performance'. In[8] other words, if students did degree level courses they should be awarded degrees. To implement this principle the Committee proposed that the National Council for Technological Awards, which was no longer needed, 'should be replaced by a Council for National Academic Awards, covering the whole of Great Britain'.[9] This recommendation also was accepted by the Government. The CNAA was established by Royal Charter in September 1964:

> with powers to award degrees, diplomas, certificates and other academic awards to persons who have successfully pursued courses of study approved by the Council at educational establishments other than universities or who have successfully carried out research work under the supervision of an educational or research establishment other than a university.

The CNAA awards Honours and Ordinary first degrees of Bachelor of Arts (B.A.) and Bachelor of Science (B.Sc.), and the higher degrees of Master of Arts (M.A.), Master of Science (M.Sc.), Master of Philosophy (M.Phil), and Doctor of Philosophy (Ph.D.). Most of the courses leading to first degrees are four-year sandwich courses which include at least one year, and frequently more, of industrial training integrated with academic study. The minimum academic qualifications required for entry into these courses in England and Wales are either the GCE with passes in five subjects including two appropriate subjects at 'A' level, or an appropriate Ordinary National Certificate at a good standard. The degrees of M.A. and M.Sc. are awarded on successful completion of courses of approved post-graduate study, those of M.Phil. and Ph.D. of programmes of original work carried out under arrangements approved by the CNAA.

In 1970 it is still too early to offer any judgment on the success of this venture. If numbers were a criterion, the CNAA has done remarkably well; its student 'population' increased fivefold—from 3000 to 15,000—between 1965 and 1969. The standard of the courses approved by the Council is said to compare favourably with that of university first-degree courses. The proportion of good degrees awarded, and the number of registrations for higher degrees both seem reasonably satisfactory. Naturally, there are teething troubles. The CNAA constitution is said to be undemocratic. Colleges complain that the interval between their submission of courses for approval and the granting of approval is unduly long. The Council's public relations are said to be poor, with the result that 'it lacks influence, prestige, and newsworthiness.[10] All, one would suggest, remediable defects.

New-style polytechnics

One still more recent, and as yet highly controversial, development in the organization of higher education must be touched upon, though at the time of writing it was only in its gestatory stage: the *Plan for Polytechnics and other colleges* which the Government announced in a White Paper published in May 1966.[11] In this Paper they said that:

> The object of developing a new pattern now is to see that the rapidly mounting demand for higher education within the system of Further Education is met in such a way as to make the best possible use of these resources without prejudicing opportunities for the tens of thousands of less advanced students who wish to take courses at intermediate and lower levels (p. 3).

[In parenthesis, this admits, as by implication the National Plan[12] had admitted in 1965, that the Robbins Committee's projection for higher education in further education establishments was a colossal underestimate. Robbins had talked in terms of 51,000 full-time and sandwich students by 1973–4, in the whole of Great Britain. The National Plan revised this to 70,000 by 1969–70. The Polytechnic White Paper revealed that by 1965 there were already 40,000 in England and Wales doing officially recognized 'advanced' studies (i.e. beyond GCE 'A' level) and a considerable number engaged on studies which (as defined above) were undoubtedly 'advanced' but had not yet been so recognized. The episode illustrates vividly the impossibility of keeping up with events in the present era of unprecedentedly rapid change.]

The Government felt that the dual demand, for advanced and non-advanced courses, could best be met by:

> concentrating full-time courses of higher education as far as practicable in a limited number of strong centres with the staff, buildings and equipment needed both to achieve and maintain high standards and to provide the right setting for an active community of staff and students.[13]

To these proposed 'strong centres' the Government gave the name 'polytechnic'—an old and honoured title now to be accorded a somewhat different meaning. The new polytechnics were, in effect, to be the comprehensive schools of higher education.

The Government believe that the best results will be achieved by developing higher education on polytechnic lines wherever practicable. This will enable staff and students to enjoy the advantages of belonging to institutions offering a wide variety of disciplines . . . a limited number of major centres in which a wider range of both full-time and part-time courses can be developed . . . comprehensive academic communities . . . expected to cater for students at all levels of higher education.[14]

The White Paper was received by most educationists with something less than enthusiasm. When the Secretary of State made detailed proposals for merging two or more neighbouring colleges 'to form a stronger and better balanced unit' he encountered open hostility from numerous further education teachers, who feared that 'merging' would mean for their colleges 'submerging'. The Secretary nevertheless adhered to his plan: but preparations for the establishment of the polytechnics were protracted, and by the autumn of 1969 were still uncompleted.

Industrial training

What might be Britain's most important venture yet in the field of vocational further education is at the time of writing only just getting under way: the compulsory national scheme laid out in the Industrial Training Act 1964. The objects of this Act are:

1. To secure an adequate supply of properly trained men and women at all levels in industry;
2. to secure an improvement in the quality and efficiency of industrial training;
3. to share the cost of training more evenly between firms.

Briefly, the scheme is as follows. The Ministry of Labour (later, Department of Employment and Productivity) has statutory power to set up for an industry, or group of related industries (e.g. engineering), an 'industrial training board'. This board is responsible for ensuring that both the quantity and the quality of the training provided in its industry or industries are adequate to meet the needs of employees at all levels. Each board has a statutory *duty* to impose a financial levy on employers, and has *powers* to pay grants to those who

actually undertake training or make arrangements for having it done. Each board determines the rate of levy for its own group.
In respect of training, a board has two principal duties:

1. To publish to its industry recommendations about the nature, content, and length of suitable courses.
2. To ensure that adequate facilities are available for the required training.

'Training' is understood to include whatever further education is deemed desirable for any particular employment. This is held to be particularly important for young employees: 'The Minister of Labour will normally refuse to approve a grant scheme unless it is a condition of grant that all young people receiving substantial training are given day release or the equivalent to take a course of further education.'[15]
The principal objectives of the further education associated with a training course are:

1. To provide the knowledge and appreciation of techniques necessary to enable a trainee to do his job;
2. to inculcate a broad understanding of relevant science and technology, so that the trainee appreciates the problems of those working in associated occupations, and is better equipped to adjust to the changes in the nature of his own work;
3. to widen a trainee's understanding of the society in which he lives, and to develop him as a person;
4. to prepare suitable trainees for more advanced study leading to more highly skilled work.

By the end of 1969 twenty-eight boards, covering the industrial training and education of nearly seventeen million employees, had been set up. There will be ultimately about thirty boards, which together will cover practically the whole of industry and commerce. This will place an extremely heavy load on colleges of further education at all levels. In crude numbers of students it could mean a four-fold increase. Moreover, it is anticipated that in many cases the colleges will be asked to provide some (possibly a large part) of the industrial training required by employees, as well as the studies defined above as 'education'. This means that further education could become for LEAs as large an enterprise as primary and secondary education, and a much more costly one. That would raise immense and complex problems of every kind, but most acutely of manpower: how to find, train, and deploy the huge army of teachers and instructors that would be needed. None of these problems is new; our country, and every other country, has been living with them for the last quarter of a century. They are the inevitable consequences of the 'education explosion', the sudden realization by the world at large that man must educate himself or perish. If we can solve these problems successfully, it will mean that virtually the entire working population, as well as all our children, will have continuously available skilled assistance in adapting to the ever-changing demands of a technological society.

Youth service

It would be gratifying, but dishonest, to suggest that the postwar years have seen substantial advance in the fields of non-vocational adult education and of the service of youth. Dissatisfaction with the lack of progress in the latter led to the outspoken Albemarle Report[16] of 1960. The Introduction to this declared that:

> We have been struck by the unanimity of evidence from witnesses (and their views were borne out by our own observations) . . .
> (i) that the Youth Service is at present in a state of acute depression.

This Report certainly provided a shot in the arm for the Youth Service; on its publication the Government at once announced an increased grant for buildings and the speedy establishment of a permanent college for the training of youth leaders. The college was opened at Leicester in 1961 (and of all unbelievable omissions was not included in the Leicester University ATO, despite McNair's persuasive pleading for parity between teachers and youth leaders!) In isolation, it has done a good job, but a single small college producing annually a few score full-time leaders can only scratch the surface of a problem affecting at the least two million young people—possibly many more. A London Report published in 1967[17] queried the youth service age limits of fourteen to twenty. In 1969 a Report by the Youth Service Development Council[18] went even farther, recommending the replacement of the Youth Service by a Youth and Community Service designed to meet the needs of children and adults.

It may well be that the conventional concept of the Youth Service, and some if not all of its varied manifestations—from the heavily programmed to the self-consciously go-as-you-please—are already obsolescent if not obsolete. Certainly, the developments which have made most rapid progress during the past few years are based on a different concept: that of service *by* young people, not of services provided *for* them by others. The idea is, of course, as old as the hills, and all voluntary youth organizations make use of it in practice. But something of a new look has been given to it by a number of national organizations which have sprung into being solely to enable young people to give organized voluntary aid, to the old, the infirm, the disabled and the destitute in particular, and the community in general in a wide variety of ways: Community Service Volunteers (CSV) and Task Force, for example; and, with a wider geographical range, but the same basic purpose, Voluntary Service Overseas (VSO) and International Volunteer Service (IVS).

In 1967 the Government decided to take a hand in this movement. In November they announced the forthcoming establishment of a new national body, the Young Volunteer Force Foundation, intended to coordinate the various efforts of young people to aid the community. At the time of writing it is too early to estimate what success this Governmentally sponsored venture is likely to command. Even its plans are vague. The Foundation is, apparently, to be administered by a Trust on which members of the three main political parties will sit. Financially, the Government is 'priming the pump' with £100,000 spread over the first three years, after which they hope private philanthropy will carry on—and presumably the Foundation will become just one of the numerous grant-aided voluntary organizations for youth. The scheme, in so far as it has been expounded, seems to resemble that of Task Force, whose director, Anthony Steen, is the first director of the new Foundation. Other youth organizations seem to be deferring judgment on this new arrival in their fold, which is probably the wisest course to take.

Spare-time University

By the middle of 1969 plans were well advanced for what may prove to be Britain's greatest experiment in non-vocational adult education: the 'Open University', which received its charter in 1969, and is due to commence operations in January 1971. The first official outline of this project was given in a White Paper, *A University of the Air*,[19] published in February 1966. By March 1968 a planning committee had decided that in addition to radio and television the Open University would make use also of correspondence courses, residential weekends and summer schools, and would arrange a tutorial system. The University would provide a wide variety of courses, but, as its name suggests, would regard courses leading to degrees as its central activity. What size or quality of response from students there will be,

163

or what the effect of the University upon existing bodies providing adult education will be only the future will reveal.

Participation

The year 1968 may well be regarded by future generations as among the most memorable years in the history of education throughout the world, as the year in which the demand of students to participate in the control and direction of their studies first became widely vocal, and, unhappily, in many countries violent. In England and Wales there was relatively little violence of any kind, and almost no extreme violence. But physical confrontations of considerable duration took place in three distinguished institutions of higher education: the University of London School of Economics and Political Science, and the art colleges at Guildford in Surrey and Hornsey in north London. Only fools would rush in with judgments on these happenings; the rest of us can only regret that the matters at issue were not resolved long ago, before they became matters of conflict. How they will ultimately be resolved only the future will tell.

The problems left for the future to solve are—as always—legion. The century briefly surveyed in this book has been educationally one of great growth and even greater advance. We have moved right out of sight of the situation Forster had to face when he introduced his Elementary Education Bill. But words he spoke upon that historic Tuesday, the 17th of February 1870, remain today as true as then:

> Upon this speedy provision of education depends also our national power. Civilized communities throughout the world are massing themselves together, each mass being measured by its force; and if we are to hold our position among men of our own race or among the nations of the world we must make up the smallness of our numbers by increasing the intellectual force of the individual.

Notes

1. Report of the Prime Minister's Committee on *Higher Education* (the Robbins Report), HMSO, 1963, p. 8.
2. *Higher Education*, p. 151, paras. 463 and 464. (*Italics mine.*)
3. W. B. Gallie. *A New University. A. D. Lindsay and the Keele experiment*, Chatto & Windus, 1960, p. 55. I am greatly indebted to Professor Gallie's account, though as I was acquainted with several of the original members of the college staff, including Lindsay, I knew the outline of the story before.

4. *University Development 1957–1962*. HMSO, 1964. Questions (not numbered) on p. 42, discussion of pattern, pp. 93–4.
5. *University Development 1957–62*, pp. 96 and 97.
6. *Higher Education*, p. 281, Recommendation 56.
7. *Ibid.*, p. 141, para. 429.
8. Report, page 8.
9. Report, p. 142.
10. 'Astryx' in *The Times Educational Supplement*, 28 February 1969.
11. Command 3006.
12. Command 2764, HMSO, 1965.
13. *Plan for Polytechnics and other colleges*, p. 3.
14. *Ibid.*, p. 5.
15. *Industrial Training and Education.* No. 35 of the 'Reports on Education' issued by the Department of Education and Science. 25 April 1967.
16. *The Youth Service in England and Wales. Report of the Committee appointed by the Minister of Education*, Command 929, February 1960. Chairman, The Countess of Albemarle.
17. *Report of a Study Group on the Youth Service in London*, ILEA, County Hall, London, SE1.
18. *Youth and Community Work in the 70s*. HMSO, October 1969.
19. Command 2922.

Bibliography

Like the text, this bibliography is a very personal affair. Many of the books mentioned in it would appear in the bibliography of any history of English education during the past century. Some would rarely if ever appear. Hundreds of books not listed here could have been included. Of those that are I will simply say, first, that they have been of help to me, and secondly, that almost all of them are easily accessible, in educational or other libraries.

General history

BOLITHO, HECTOR. *The Reign of Queen Victoria.* Collins, 1949.
BRUCE, MAURICE. *The Coming of the Welfare State.* Batsford, 1961.
BRYANT, ARTHUR. *English Saga 1840–1940.* Collins, 1940.
GRAVES, ROBERT, and HODGE, ALAN. *The Long Week-End. A social history of Great Britain, 1918–1939.* Faber, 1940.
HALÉVY, ELIE. *History of the English People. Epilogue.* Vol. I: *1895–1905*, Book II. (Transl. E. I. Watkin.) Penguin Books, 1939. (First published in English, 1926.)
JONES, IDRIS. *Modern Welsh History. From 1485 to the present day.* Bell, 1948.
THOMSON, DAVID. *England in the Nineteenth Century 1815–1914.* Penguin Books, 1950.
—— *England in the Twentieth Century 1914–1963.* Penguin Books, 1965.
TREVELYAN, G. M. *British History in the Nineteenth Century and After.* Longmans, 1922.
—— *English Social History.* Longmans, 1944.
YOUNG, G. M. *Portrait of an Age. Victorian England.* Oxford University Press, 1936.

Histories of education

ADAMSON, J. W. *English Education 1789–1902.* Cambridge University Press, 1930.

ARCHER, R. L. *Secondary Education in the Nineteenth Century.* Cambridge University Press, 1937.

ARGLES, MICHAEL. *South Kensington to Robbins. An account of English technical and scientific education since 1851.* Longmans, 1964.

ARMYTAGE, W. H. G. *Four Hundred Years of English Education.* Cambridge University Press, 1964.

—— *Civic Universities.* Benn, 1955.

BALFOUR, GRAHAM. *The Educational Systems of Great Britain and Ireland.* Oxford: Clarendon Press, 1898.

BARNARD, H. C. *A History of English Education from 1760,* 2nd edn. University of London Press, 1961.

BIRCHENOUGH, CHARLES. *History of Elementary Education in England and Wales from 1800 to the present day,* 3rd edn., University Tutorial Press, 1938.

BOYD, WILLIAM and RAWSON, WYATT. *The Story of the New Education.* Heinemann, 1965.

CARDWELL, D. S. L. *The Organisation of Science in England.* Heinemann, 1957.

CRUICKSHANK, M. *Church and State in English Education. 1870 to the present day.* Macmillan, 1963.

CURTIS, S. J. *History of Education in Great Britain,* 6th edn. University Tutorial Press, 1965.

EAGLESHAM, E. J. R. *From School Board to Local Authority.* Routledge & Kegan Paul, 1956.

—— *The Foundations of 20th Century Education in England.* Routledge & Kegan Paul, 1967.

KAMM, JOSEPHINE. *Hope Deferred. Girls' education in English history.* Methuen, 1965.

LOWNDES, G. A. N. *The Silent Social Revolution.* Oxford University Press, 1937.

MACK, E. C. *Public Schools and British Opinion.* Vol. I, 1780 to 1860, Methuen, 1938. Vol. II, Since 1860, Columbia University Press, 1941.

MACLURE, J. STUART. *Educational Documents. England and Wales 1816–1963.* Chapman & Hall, 1965.

OSBORNE, G. S. *Scottish and English Schools. A comprehensive survey of the past fifty years.* Longmans, 1966.

PRITCHARD, F. C. *Methodist Secondary Education.* Epworth Press, 1949.

SIMON, BRIAN. *History of Education 1780–1870*. Lawrence & Wishart, 1960.

—— *Education and the Labour Movement 1870–1918*. Lawrence & Wishart, 1965.

SMITH, FRANK. *A History of English Elementary Education 1760–1902*. University of London Press, 1931.

SMITH, W. O. LESTER. *To Whom do Schools Belong?* 2nd edn. Blackwell, 1945.

—— *Education in Great Britain*. 5th edn. Oxford University Press, 1967.

STEWART, W. A. C. *The Educational Innovators*. Vol. 2. *Progressive Schools 1881–1967*. Macmillan, 1968.

STEWART, W. A. C. and MCCANN, W. P. *The Educational Innovators 1750–1880*. Macmillan, 1967.

Biographical works

ALLEN, B. M. *Sir Robert Morant. A great public servant*. Macmillan, 1934.

ASHBY, M. K. *Joseph Ashby of Tysoe, 1859–1919*. Cambridge University Press, 1961.

BADLEY, J. H. *Memories and Reflections*. Allen & Unwin, 1955.

BATTERSBY, W. J. *Brother Potamian, Educator and Scientist*. Burns Oates, 1953.

BAZELEY, E. T. *Homer Lane and the Little Commonwealth*. Allen & Unwin, 1928.

BEACOCK, D. A. *Play Way English for To-day. The methods and influence of H. Caldwell Cook*. Nelson, 1943.

CHOLMONDELEY, ESSEX. *The Story of Charlotte Mason, 1842–1923*. Dent, 1960.

CLARK, LEONARD, ed. *The Kingdom of the Mind. Essays and addresses 1903–37 of Albert Mansbridge*. Dent, 1944.

CONNELL, W. F. *The Educational Thought and Influence of Matthew Arnold*. Routledge & Kegan Paul, 1950.

CRESSWELL, D'ARCY. *Margaret McMillan. A memoir*. Hutchinson, 1948.

DAVIES, RUPERT, ed. *John Scott Lidgett. A symposium*. Epworth Press, 1957.

FISHER, H. A. L. *An Unfinished Autobiography*. Oxford University Press, 1940.

GITTINS, C. and others. *Pioneers of Welsh Education. Four Lectures*. Faculty of Education, University College, Swansea, 1965.

GORELL, LORD. *One Man . . . Many Parts*. Odhams, 1956.

GRIER, LYNDA. *Achievement in Education. The work of Michael Ernest Sadler 1885–1935.* Constable, 1952.

HARTOG, LADY MABEL. *P. J. Hartog. A memoir by his wife.* Constable, 1949.

HEARL, T. W. *William Barnes 1801–1886. The schoolmaster. A study of education in the life and work of the Dorset poet.* Printed by Longmans (Dorchester) Ltd., 1966.

HOPKINSON, DIANA. *Family Inheritance. A Life of Eva Hubback.* Staples Press, 1954.

IREMONGER, F. A. *William Temple, Archbishop of Canterbury. His life and letters.* Oxford University Press, 1948.

JUDGES, A. V., ed. *Pioneers of English Education.* Faber, 1953.

KAMM, JOSEPHINE. *How Different from Us. A biography of Miss Buss and Miss Beale.* Bodley Head, 1958.

KEKEWICH, SIR G. W. *The Education Department and After.* Constable, 1920.

LAWRENCE, EVELYN, ed. *Friedrich Froebel and English Education.* University of London Press, 1952.

LOWNDES, G. A. N. *Margaret McMillan. 'The Children's Champion'.* Museum Press, 1960.

MANSBRIDGE, ALBERT. *Fellow Men. A gallery of England 1876–1946.* Dent, 1948.

MITCHELL, F. W. *Sir Fred Clarke. Master-teacher 1880–1952.* Longmans, 1967.

NEILL, A. S. *Summerhill. A radical approach to education.* Gollancz, 1962.

PEACOCK, ROGER S. *Pioneer of Boyhood. Story of Sir William A. Smith, founder of the Boys' Brigade.* Boys' Brigade, 1954.

REID, T. WEMYSS. *Life of the Rt. Hon. William Edward Forster.* Chapman & Hall, 1888.

REITH, J. C. W. (LORD). *Into the Wind.* Hodder & Stoughton, 1949.

RIDLER, ANNE. *Olive Willis and Downe House: an adventure in education.* Murray, 1967.

SILBER, KATE. *Pestalozzi. The man and his work.* Routledge & Kegan Paul, 1960.

SIMPSON, J. H. *Schoolmaster's Harvest. Some findings of fifty years, 1894–1944.* Faber, 1954.

Spencer Leeson: Shepherd: Teacher: Friend. A Memoir by some of his friends. S.P.C.K., 1958.

STANDING, E. M. *Maria Montessori. Her life and work.* Hollis & Carter, 1957.

WALLER, R. D., ed. *Harold Pilkington Turner. Memories of his work and personality.* Manchester University Press, 1953.

WILLS, D. W. *Homer Lane: a biography.* Allen & Unwin, 1964.

YOUNG, RUTH. *The Life of an educational worker (Henrietta Busk).* Longmans, 1934.

Sociological studies

ARNOLD, MATTHEW. *Culture and Anarchy.* Smith, Elder, 1869; 2nd, much revised, edn., 1875.

BALLARD, P. B. *The Changing School.* University of London Press, 1925.

BANTOCK, G. H. *Education in an Industrial Society.* Faber, 1963.

BARON, G. *Society, Schools and Progress in England.* Pergamon, 1965.

BERNBAUM, G. *Social Change and the Schools 1918–1944.* Routledge & Kegan Paul, 1967.

CARTER, M. P. *Home, School and Work. A study of the education and employment of young people in Britain.* Pergamon, 1962.

CLARKE, F. *Education and Social Change. An English interpretation.* Sheldon Press, 1940.

DOUGLAS, J. W. B. *The Home and the School. A study of ability and attainment in the primary school.* MacGibbon and Kee, 1964.

DOUGLAS, J. W. B., ROSS, J. M. and SIMPSON, H. R. *All our future. A longitudinal study of secondary education.* Peter Davies, 1968.

ELVIN, H. L. *Education and Contemporary Society.* Watts, 1965.

EVANS, OWEN E. *Redeeming the Time. A survey of the Junior Instruction Centre Movement.* Liverpool University Press, 1941.

FLOUD, J. E., ed. *Social Class and Educational Opportunity.* Heinemann, 1956.

GLASS, D. V., ed. *Social Mobility in Britain.* Routledge & Kegan Paul, 1954.

GOODWIN, M., ed. *Nineteenth Century Opinion. An anthology of extracts from the first fifty volumes of 'The Nineteenth Century' 1877–1901.* Penguin Books, 1951.

HOGGART, RICHARD. *The Uses of Literacy.* Chatto & Windus, 1957.

HOLMES, EDMOND. *What Is and What Might Be. A study of education in general and elementary education in particular.* Constable, 1912.

JACKSON, BRIAN and MARSDEN, DENNIS. *Education and the Working Class. Some general themes raised by a study of 88 working-class children in a northern industrial city.* Routledge & Kegan Paul, 1962.

JAHODA, MARIE. *The Education of Technologists. An exploratory case study at Brunel College.* Tavistock Publications, 1963.

LEWIS, ROY and MAUDE, ANGUS. *The English Middle Classes.* Phoenix House, 1949.

—— *Professional People.* Phoenix House, 1952.

LUSH, A. J. *The Young Adult in South Wales.* University of Wales Press, 1941.

MANNHEIM, KARL. *Diagnosis of Our Time. War-time Essays of a Sociologist.* Kegan Paul, Trench, & Trubner, 1943.

MÉGROZ, R. L. *Pedagogues are Human.* Rockliff, 1950.

MUSGRAVE, P. W. *Society and Education in England since 1800.* Methuen, 1968.

NORWOOD, CYRIL. *The English Tradition of Education.* Murray, 1929.

SIMON, BRIAN, ed. *New Trends in English Education.* MacGibbon and Kee, 1957.

WEBB, BEATRICE. *Our Partnership,* edited by Barbara Drake, and Margaret Cole. Longmans, 1948.

WILLIAMS, RAYMOND. *Culture and Society 1780–1950.* Chatto & Windus, 1958.

—— *The Long Revolution.* Chatto & Windus, 1961.

YOUNG, MICHAEL. *The Rise of the Meritocracy. An essay on education and equality.* Thames and Hudson, 1958.

The educational system

ALEXANDER, SIR WILLIAM. *Education in England. The national system—how it works,* 2nd edn. Newnes Educational, 1964.

BURGESS, TYRELL. *A Guide to English Schools.* Penguin Books, 1964.

DENT, H. C. *The Educational System of England and Wales,* 4th edn. University of London Press, 1969.

KOERNER, JAMES D. *Reform in Education, England and the United States.* Weidenfeld & Nicolson, 1968.

Government and administration

BINGHAM, J. H. *The Period of the Sheffield School Board 1870–1903.* Sheffield: J. W. Northend Ltd, 1949.

DENT, H. C. *The Education Act 1944. Provisions, Regulations, Circulars, Later Acts,* 12th edn. University of London Press, 1968.

EDMONDS, E. L. *The First Headship.* Basil Blackwell, 1968.

GOSDEN, P. H. J. H. *The Development of Educational Administration in England and Wales.* Basil Blackwell, 1966.

TAYLOR, G. and SAUNDERS, J. B., eds. *The New Law of Education,* 6th edn. Butterworth, 1965.

Stages and types of education

Primary education

BOARD OF EDUCATION. *Handbook of Suggestions for the consideration of Teachers and others engaged in the Work of Public Elementary Schools.* HMSO, first published, 1905.

CONSULTATIVE COMMITTEE OF THE BOARD OF EDUCATION. *The Primary School.* HMSO, 1931.

—— *Infant and Nursery Schools.* HMSO, 1933.

MINISTRY OF EDUCATION. *Primary Education. Suggestions for the consideration of teachers and others concerned with the work of primary schools.* HMSO, 1959.

CENTRAL ADVISORY COUNCIL FOR EDUCATION (ENGLAND). *Children and their Primary Schools* (The Plowden Report). Vol. I, Report, Vol. II, Research and Surveys. HMSO, 1967.

CENTRAL ADVISORY COUNCIL FOR EDUCATION (WALES). *Primary Education in Wales.* (The Gittins Report). HMSO, 1968.

DEARDEN, R. F. *The Philosophy of Primary Education.* Routledge & Kegan Paul, 1968.

MASTERS, PHILIP L. *Preparatory Schools Today. Some facts and inferences.* A. and C. Black, 1966.

ROSS, A. M. *The Education of Childhood.* Harrap, 1960.

Secondary education

CONSULTATIVE COMMITTEE OF THE BOARD OF EDUCATION. *Differentiation of Curricula between the Sexes in Secondary Schools.* HMSO, 1923.

—— *The Education of the Adolescent* (The Hadow Report). HMSO, 1926.

—— *Secondary Education, with special reference to Grammar Schools and Technical High Schools* (The Spens Report). HMSO, 1938.

SECONDARY SCHOOL EXAMINATIONS COUNCIL. *Curriculum and Examinations in Secondary Schools* (The Norwood Report). HMSO, 1943.

BOARD OF EDUCATION. *The Public Schools and the General Educational System* (The Fleming Report). HMSO, 1944. This was preceded in 1943 by a 'Special Report' (by the same committee) on *Abolition of Tuition Fees in Grant-Aided Secondary Schools.*

CENTRAL ADVISORY COUNCIL ON EDUCATION (ENGLAND). *Early Leaving.* HMSO, 1954.

—— *Half our Future* (The Newsom Report). HMSO, 1963.

PUBLIC SCHOOLS COMMISSION. *The Public Schools Commission: First Report,* Vol. I. HMSO, 1968.

BANKS, OLIVE. *Parity and Prestige in English Secondary Education.* Routledge & Kegan Paul, 1955.

COLE, ROGER. *Comprehensive Schools in Action.* Oldbourne, 1964.

EDWARDS, REESE. *The Secondary Technical School.* University of London Press, 1960.

KALTON, GRAHAM. *Public Schools. A factual survey.* Longmans, 1966.

NATIONAL UNION OF TEACHERS, ed. *Inside the Comprehensive School. A symposium contributed by heads of comprehensive schools in England and Wales.* Schoolmaster Publishing Co., 1958.

OGILVIE, VERNON. *The English Public School.* Batsford, 1957.

PASSOW, A. HARRY. *Secondary Education for All. The English approach.* Ohio State University Press, 1961.

STEVENS, FRANCES. *The Living Tradition. The social and educational assumptions of the grammar school.* Hutchinson, 1960.

TAWNEY, R. H., ed. *Secondary Education for All. A policy for Labour.* Allen & Unwin, for the Labour Party, 1922.

TAYLOR, WILLIAM. *The Secondary Modern School.* Faber, 1963.

Special education

DUNCAN, JOHN. *The Education of the Ordinary Child. Lankhills Methods.* Nelson, 1942.

PRITCHARD, D. G. *Education and the Handicapped 1760–1960.* Routledge & Kegan Paul, 1963.

SEGAL, S. S. *No Child is Ineducable. Special education—provisions and trends.* Pergamon, 1967.

Further education

BREW, J. MACALISTER. *In the Service of Youth. A practical manual of work among adolescents.* Faber, 1943.

CENTRAL ADVISORY COUNCIL ON EDUCATION (ENGLAND). *15–18.* (The Crowther Report). Vol. I, Report; Vol. II, Surveys. HMSO, 1959, 1960.

HARRISON, J. F. C. *Learning and Living 1790–1960. A study in the history of the English adult education movement.* Routledge & Kegan Paul, 1961.

HAWKINS, G. and WALLER, R. D., eds. *A Design for Democracy. An abridgment of a Report of the Adult Education Committee of the British Ministry of Reconstruction commonly called the 1919 Report.* Max Parrish, 1956.

HAWKINS, T. H. and BRIMBLE, L. J. F. *Adult Education: The record of the British Army.* Macmillan, 1946.

JAMES, DAVID, ed. *Outward Bound.* Routledge & Kegan Paul, 1957.

KITCHEN, P. I. *From Learning to Earning. Birth and growth of a Young People's College.* Faber, 1944.

MANSBRIDGE, A. *An Adventure in Working-Class Education.* Longmans, 1920.

MORGAN, A. E. *The Needs of Youth. A report made to King George's Jubilee Trust Fund.* Oxford University Press, 1939.

PEERS, ROBERT. *Adult Education. A comprehensive Study.* Routledge & Kegan Paul, 1958.

PETERS, A. J. *British Further Education. A critical textbook.* Pergamon, 1967.

PRICE, T. W. *The Story of the Workers' Educational Association 1903–24.* The Labour Publishing Co., 1924.

PRIME MINISTER'S COMMITTEE. *Higher Education* (The Robbins Report). Report and 5 Appendices, HMSO, 1963.

VENABLES, P. F. R. *Technical Education. Its aims, organisation and future development.* Bell, 1955.

University education

BERDAHL, ROBERT O. *British Universities and the State.* University of California Press; Cambridge University Press, 1959.

DENT, H. C. *Universities in Transition.* Cohen & West (Routledge & Kegan Paul), 1961.

FLEXNER, ABRAHAM. *Universities American, English, German.* Oxford University Press, 1930.

MOBERLY, SIR WALTER. *The Crisis in the University.* SCM Press, 1949.

MOUNTFORD, SIR JAMES. *British Universities.* Oxford University Press, 1966.

NEWMAN, J. H. *The Idea of a University.* First published 1852, revised and enlarged 1873. New edn., ed. C. F. Harrold. Longmans, 1947.

TRUSCOT, BRUCE. *Redbrick University.* Faber, 1943.

UNIVERSITY GRANTS COMMITTEE. *Returns from Universities and University Colleges in Receipt of Treasury* Grant.* (Annually since 1920–21). HMSO.

—— *Annual Survey.* Published with the *Returns* from 1958–59 to 1961–62, and separately since. HMSO.

—— *University Development.* (A survey published ordinarily every five years.) HMSO.

There are published histories of all the universities except some of the very youngest. In the case of Oxford, Cambridge, and London there are also histories of constituent colleges.

* From 1962–3, 'Exchequer'.

Teachers and teacher training

JONES, LANCE G. E. *The Training of Teachers in England and Wales. A critical survey.* Oxford University Press, 1924.

NATIONAL UNION OF TEACHERS. *The Training of Teachers and Grants to Intending Teachers.* NUT, 1939.

RICH, R. W. *The Training of Teachers in England and Wales during the Nineteenth Century.* Cambridge University Press, 1933.

RICHARDSON, C. A. and others. *The education of teachers in England, France and U.S.A.* Unesco, 1953.

TAYLOR, W. *Society and the Education of Teachers.* Faber, 1969.

TRAINING COLLEGE ASSOCIATION and COUNCIL OF PRINCIPALS. *The Training of Teachers.* University of London Press, 1939.

TROPP, ASHER. *The School Teachers. The growth of the teaching profession in England and Wales from 1800 to the present day.* Heinemann, 1957.

There are unfortunately very few published histories of training colleges and university departments of education. Culham, Doncaster (*Our Present Opportunities*, O. M. Stanton), Goldsmiths (*The Forge*, ed. Dorothy Dymond), Lincoln, Sheffield, and Westminster are among the most substantial.

Audio visual aids

EDUCATIONAL FOUNDATION FOR VISUAL AIDS. *Survey of British research in audio-visual aids.* National Committee for Audio-Visual Aids in Education, 1965.

LEEDHAM, J. and UNWIN, D. *Programmed Learning in the Schools.* Longmans, 1965.

NATIONAL COMMITTEE FOR AUDIO-VISUAL AIDS IN EDUCATION. *Closed Circuit Television in Education.* Report of the Experimental Development Unit. National Committee for Audio-Visual Aids in Education, 1965.

PALMER, RICHARD. *School Broadcasting in Britain.* BBC, 1947.

Examinations

BRERETON, J. L. *The Case for Examinations. An account of their place in education, with some proposals for their reform.* Cambridge University Press, 1944.

MINISTRY OF EDUCATION (SSEC). *Secondary School Examinations other than the G.C.E.* (The Beloe Report). HMSO, 1960.

MONTGOMERY, R. J. *Examinations. An account of their evolution as administrative devices in England.* Longmans, 1965.
VERNON, P. E. *The Measurement of Abilities*, 2nd edn. University of London Press, 1956.
VERNON, P. E., ed. *Secondary School Selection. A British psychological Society inquiry.* Methuen, 1957.

Finance

DEPARTMENT OF EDUCATION AND SCIENCE. *Statistics of Education.* Annually. First published 1961 : previously included in the Department's Annual Report. HMSO.
VAIZEY, JOHN. *The Costs of Education.* Allen & Unwin, 1958.
—— *The Economics of Education.* Faber, 1962.

Inspection

EDMONDS, E. L. *The School Inspector.* Routledge & Kegan Paul, 1962.
LEESE, JOHN. *Personalities and Power in English Education.* Arnold, 1950.

Theory

ADAMS, JOHN. *The Evolution of Educational Theory.* Macmillan, 1912.
NUNN, PERCY. *Education, Its Data and First Principles.* Arnold, 1920.
RUSSELL, BERTRAND, (EARL). *On Education especially in early childhood.* Allen & Unwin, 1926.
TIBBLE, J. W. ed. *The Study of Education.* Routledge & Kegan Paul, 1966.
WHITEHEAD, A. N. *The Aims of Education and other essays.* Williams & Norgate, 1932.

Government publications

Annual, periodical, and occasional.

All current and many recent Government publications are obtainable through booksellers or direct from the publishers, Her Majesty's Stationery Office, at 49 High Holborn, London, WC1, or in Birmingham, Bristol, Cardiff, Manchester, Edinburgh and Belfast.
Annual Reports of the Committee of the Privy Council on Education, 1840–1899.
Annual Reports of the Board of Education, 1900–1938.

Annual Reports of the Ministry of Education, 1947–63.
Annual Reports of the Department of Education and Science, 1964–.
Biennial Reports of the Chief Medical Officer. Formerly annual. Started 1908.
Teachers' salaries. Reports are published after all agreements made by the Burnham, Pelham, or other negotiating committees.
Reports on education. Four-page broadsheets each dealing with a single aspect or branch of the educational service. Issued monthly (gratis). Started July 1963.
Educational pamphlets. Longer studies, also dealing with single topics. By 1969 about fifty had been published since 1944.

Bibliographical and reference

FOSTER, J. F. and CRAIG, T., eds. *Commonwealth Universities Year Book.* Association of Commonwealth Universities. First published 1914.
ATCDE. *Handbook of Colleges and Departments of Education 1968.* (Successor to *Handbook on Training for Teaching*, first published 1954.) Methuen, 1968. Revised periodically.
BARNARD, H. C. and LAUWERYS, J. A. *A Handbook of British Educational Terms, including an outline of the British educational system.* Harrap, 1963.
BARON, G. *A Bibliographical Guide to the English Educational System*, 3rd edn. Athlone Press (University of London), 1965.
BURNET, J. F., ed. *The Public and Preparatory Schools Year Book.* A. and C. Black.
BURTON, M. A., ed. *The Girls' School Year Book.* A. and C. Black.
—— *The Independent Schools Association Year Book.* A. and C. Black.
DENT, H. C., ed. *The Year Book of Technical Education and Training for Industry.* A. and C. Black. Started 1957.
DEPARTMENT OF EDUCATION AND SCIENCE. *A Compendium of Teacher Training Courses in England and Wales* (List 172). Annually. HMSO.
—— *Education Committee's Year Book.* Councils and Education Press.
—— *The Education Authorities' Directory and Annual.* School Government Publishing Co.

Periodicals

Education. Journal of the Association of Education Committees. Councils and Education Press, 10 Queen Anne Street, London, W1. Started 1903.

The Schoolmaster (from 1963 *The Teacher*). Journal of the National Union of Teachers. Derbyshire House, St. Chad's Street, London, WC1. Started 1871.

The Times Educational Supplement. Times Newspapers Ltd, Printing House Square, London, EC4. Started 1910.

Universities Quarterly. Turnstile Press, 10 Great Turnstile, London, WC1.

Index

Robbins